The Build

Leadership Builds:
God's Churches, Ministries, and Your Life.

Phillip Baker

Copyright © 2019 by Phillip Baker.

All rights reserved.

No part of this publication may be used, reproduced, distributed or transmitted in any form or by any means, including photocopying, recording, or other electronic or mechanical methods, without the prior written permission from:

Phillip Baker Ministries
P.O. Box 1708
Dickinson, Texas 77539
www.phillipbaker.org

Scripture marked (KJV) are taken from The Holy Bible King James Version. Accessed on Bible Gateway. www.BibleGateway.com

Book Layout ©2019 BookDesignTemplates.com

The Build - Leadership Builds:God's Churches, Ministries, and Your Life/Phillip Baker. —1st ed.

ISBN 9798392561209

Endorsements

"PBM is a dynamite of a ministry in equipping the churches of today to become Kingdom builders. Phillip and PBM's heart towards people equates to that of Jesus wanting to see them whole; spirit, soul and body. Because of this, we intentionally connected and partnered with PBM to see this same heart of transforming and training leaders of this generation to impact our nation. Phillip is family to us here at church and we witnessed him many times pouring God's Presence through his teachings."
Pastors Francis (Jim) & Jeng Yap
Come to Jesus Church
Sydney, Australia

"I know Phillip Baker as a person who is an example of a servant of Jesus Christ. His love and passion for God's church makes him travel all over the world, including Bulgaria. As he travels he takes part in the growth of the churches he visits and trains their leadership to be fully in God's call. I am amazed by the passion and energy with which he serves. This is an inspiration and encouragement for me and the leadership of our church."
Pastor Ognyan Serafimov
New Generation Church
Sophia, Bulgaria

"Bro. Phillip Baker always leaves our church better than when he got there. PBM has been so influential in helping stir the God-given mandate on our church. PBM truly loves the church and the church truly loves PBM."
Pastor Jaime Gonzalez
World Harvest Family Church
Edinburg, Texas

"Phillip is a student of personal growth and development. Phillip believes He has the power to change us individually, connect communities, transform churches and countries around the world. His passion in life is growing and equipping others to do remarkable things and lead significant and fulfilled lives."

Pastor Jimmy Davis
Grace Tabernacle
Buffalo, Texas

"This practical and tested leadership resource will help every pastor and leader create a culture of effectiveness. Phillip's heart for pastors, leaders, and churches to be healthy and expand God's Kingdom flows out of every principle and page. Don't just read it, apply it!"

Pastor Doug Bartsch,
HIS Place Family Church
Spring, Texas

"At New Life Church, we love Phillip Baker! His leadership teachings and writings have impacted our leaders for many years. His love for the local church is apparent as he communicates Kingdom principles. My prayer is that as you read this book, your capacity to lead will increase, your personal life will be strengthened, and the church will move forward."

Bishop Dave Dolan
New Life Church
Sullivan, Illinois

"Phillip Baker is a Kingdom man with a Kingdom mission and a Kingdom message. His teachings are faith building and inspirational with the purpose to build Kingdom

minded leaders in the local church. I know you will be blessed by this book."

Pastor Steven A. Smith
WestPoint Church
New Orleans, Louisiana

"Well done my good and faithful servant, Phillip epitomizes this statement. His love for the local church and desire for leaders to rise up is unparalleled. He captivates his listeners through his deep knowledge of leadership principles. He makes the church a better place."

Pastor August Patroelj
New Life Christian Church
Falfurrias, Texas

"I have known Bro. Phillip for approximately twenty years in half a dozen ministry settings. He has adjusted his approach to each setting, respecting existing l eadership authority, while thoughtfully encouraging positive change through wisdom. His no-nonsense approach to solutions brought; restoration, resolution and revolution to G.A.P. His love for the local church has enthused our gathering to love each other more."

Pastor Jim Land
G.A.P Church
Miami, Oklahoma

"Phillip Baker's love of the local church is contagious to anyone who listens. His leadership teaching empowers, equips, and enlightens believers to be who God wants them to be. Our church and myself personally have

reaped blessings from the seeds that have been dropped in our hearts!"

Pastor Josue Maldonado
New Life Assembly of God
Ft. Worth, Texas

"The statement has been quoted many times, "Everything rises or falls on Leadership". This is true and Phillip Baker Ministries and the new book "The Build" has reached the core of the Kingdom, raising up and under-girding leaders of the next great move of God."

Pastor Zack P. Mitchell
Word of Hope Church
New Iberia, Louisiana

"The ministry of Phillip Baker and his ministry has been invaluable to me as a Pastor and for my church. His heart to pour into me and come alongside me as I strive to grow in my leadership abilities and to minister to and develop leaders in the local church is unmatched in my opinion. From the very beginning of our friendship, his ministry has loved, encouraged, and challenged me as a leader and is doing incredible things for Pastors and leaders and for the Kingdom of God. Phillip is anointed to teach and to bless church leaders today."

Pastor Darin Brannon
New River Family Fellowship
Wentworth, Missouri

"Over the past 18 years I have not only had the privilege of knowing Bro. Phillip Baker but also have had the honor to sit under his extensive knowledge on leadership.

God has truly anointed Phillip with a passion for leaders that spreads through the local church like a wild fire. His teaching style will ignite a sense of ownership through your leaders that will take them from "this is the church I attend" to "this is MY church".

Dr. Corey Endsley
The Exchange Worship Center
Corpus Christi, Texas

I confidently recommend Phillip Baker Ministries to you personally and your family church congregation. Bro Phillip and his amazing family have impacted so many lives through their obedience in building the Kingdom of God and dedicated in bringing church leadership to new levels. We the body of Christ are blessed having Phillip Baker Ministries in covenant with us.

Pastor Mark Linares
Living Faith Family Worship Church
Cotulla, Texas

I've known Phillip for quite a few years now and I will have to say, he's one of the most encouraging and loving people I've ever met. Phillip is full of the Holy Spirit, full of the Word and full of love. His leadership seminars are simply phenomenal. I would highly recommend this book to you. Not only will it help you personally, but it will give you the tools you need to be a success in all you do.

Pastor Rick Becker
Thrive Church
Greenville, Tennessee

We are so thankful for the leadership skills given by Phillip Baker! These applicable, valuable skills are powerful and ministry changing. We are blessed to have a relationship with a ministry like PBM who are huge supporters of the local church, no matter the size!

Pastor Chris Larson
New Life Fellowship
Seguin, Texas

Phillip Baker's heart to build the local church and its pastors is unparalleled. For almost 20 years, he has consistently ministered to our congregation. Bro. Phillip is like a Swiss army knife when it comes to what he has to offer a church... But out of all of the different aspects of his ministry, I believe his teaching on leadership has blessed our church the most. He challenges me personally as a leader as well as the core leadership of our church every time he is with us!

Pastor Kolbe Hill
The Remnant Church
LaGrange, Texas

One phrase sums up Phillip Baker Ministries. "PBM is passionate about building the local church." From studying the early church, we learn that everything begins and ends in the local church. Phillip Baker passionately pours himself into church leaders and pastors, not only nationally but also globally. Signs, wonders, and miracles accompany this man of God as he preaches and teaches the Word of God. He always leaves churches and leaders healthier and inspires you to believe God for more and live your best days now!

Pastor Spike Maldonado
New Life Church
Amarillo, Texas

Phillip Baker is the happiest evangelist you will ever meet. I have know Phillip for many years and deeply respect who he is and all he does for the body of Christ. His words, passion, and insights encourage, challenge, and inspire people to dig deeper and dream bigger. It is exciting that he has put those stories, life lessons, and principles into this book. What a gift it will be to this generation and the next! Phillip is a blessing to pastors, to the local church, and to all who are privileged to know him. He truly is on a mission to BUILD the Kingdom of God.

Pastor Clem Garcia
Grace Temple Church
Goliad, TX

Phillip Baker Ministries has been encouraging and uplifting our church body for years. Phillip offers authentic testimony and simple guidelines that help increase your faith. Using quality time in a small group setting with our staff, Phillip equipped our leaders to continue in service with excellence. Any time PBM ministers to our congregation, we receive motivational messages to propel us forward.

Pastor Samuel Priddy
The Lord' House
Tyler, TX

Of all the contacts I know doing Kingdom work, Phillip Baker has done more to help encourage and work with pastors on building leadership in our churches. His favorite saying is leadership builds the church and the church builds the Kingdom. His ministry is to help pastors to have the vision to lead and to encourage them to build leaders in their churches. Phillip Baker actually cares about pastors and is a constant source of encouragement! You'll enjoy this book and it will help you in your ministry!

Pastor Marty Reid
Trinity Family Church
Forney, TX

The name of this book says it all. Jesus' final words were, go make disciples. BUILD LEADERS. No one does that more simplistically than PBM. Great leaders are built by great leaders in every area of life, but the heart of this ministry is the local church. Their impact on our lives have launched CCAM further and consistently into the deep, the new, and the cutting-edge of ministry.

Pastor Paul Gray
The Christian Church at Minden
World Outreach Center
Minden, LA

Dedication

I would very much like to dedicate this book to all of the Father's wonderful servants in the Kingdom and in His incredible local churches.

You are the people who show up early and stay late. You are the ones who turn on the lights to create an inviting room, adjust the thermostats so it is not too cold or too hot, and check the bathrooms for cleanliness, toilet paper and hand towels. You are the individuals who care for the grounds, pull weeds, plant new flowers yearly and overall establish the aesthetics called landscaping. You also prepare meals for events, set up the tables and chairs, cover the tables with tablecloths, take down tables and chairs, wash the dishes, and make sure the kitchen is left clean and ready for the next event. You arrive early so you can drive the van to collect those that have no way to attend church without your assistance. You are the ones who take care of the church sign, clean the church, and make coffee. You are the ones who volunteer for the nursery, pour love into children, and spend time with the teens. You are the ones who spend their vacation taking the young people to camp in the church van, traveling hours from home, and that you assisted their nonstop fundraising efforts for the last 3 months, desiring that everyone has a chance to go to camp. You are the ones who pray for the service on the way to church. You are the ones who meet people in the parking lot armed with an umbrella to escort them into the building, safe and dry. You are the smiling faces who welcome visitors when they arrive and direct them to the correct place. You are the amazing people who open their homes weekly in order for people to be discipled in a comfortable, relaxed setting. You are the ones who take care of the pastor, pray for him, and answer the phone when he calls needing assistance.

You are Kingdom servants and I dedicate The Build to YOU.

Thank you for all the many things, known and unknown, you do to move the Kingdom and His churches forward. Many servants like you may not ever get the honor and recognition that comes from being in the five fold ministry. However, many servants like you will continue to be faithful even when most people in a church do not understand or truly even know all you do. The one thing you can rest assured knowing is God knows, Jesus and the Holy Spirit know, and Heaven is making note of it all. Let me put this in the most simple of words. The Kingdom and God's churches would not be what they are today if it was not for **YOU**!

I wrote this book because you are incredibly special.
I wrote this book to say, Thank you.
I wrote this book because YOU need help.

Love you all,
Phillip Baker

TABLE OF CONTENTS

	Endorsements..........................3
	Dedications............................11
	Introduction to *THE BUILD*...............15
Chapter 1	Breaking Containment........................21
Chapter 2	Leadership Builds Builds 1-20..............................29
Chapter 3	Servant Leadership Builds 21-45............................39
Chapter 4	Supernatural Leadership Builds 46-65............................51
Chapter 5	Vision Leadership Builds 66-190...........................61
Chapter 6	Leadership Attributes Builds 91-110...........................73
Chapter 7	Precision Leadership Builds 111-130..........................83
Chapter 8	Kingdom Churches Builds 131-153..........................93
Chapter 9	Kingdom Pastors Builds 154-173.........................105
Chapter 10	Kingdom Assignments Builds 174-195.........................115
Chapter 11	The Heavenly Vision Builds 196-203.........................129

Introduction

First of all, thank you so much for choosing to spend time with this book. I hope you enjoy it, are challenged by it, and inspired to do more for the Kingdom than ever before. As you read this book, you will begin to see the thread of three words written over and over.

Kingdom
Church
Leader

Everything in this book is about building the Kingdom, building God's churches, and *you*, yes *you*, being the leader that executes the construction. I am keenly aware that the majority of books on leadership contain wisdom that will help you build a business and be successful in the workplace. *The Build* has no lack of that type of information, however, I must tell you unapologetically and with full disclosure, that *The Build* is primarily written with the above three words at the forefront of my heart and mind. *The Build* puts the Kingdom first. *The Build*, at its very core is simply a love letter to the Church. *The Build* is a gift for Pastors, in which I pray, assists them in the task of assembling and training servants and leaders, of which there is definite lack. *The Build* was written to transition believers into servants and then assist them to become Kingdom leaders, who will one day, like the Apostle Paul, be able to say according to Acts 26:19,

"I was not disobedient to the Heavenly Vision." Acts 26:19

I sincerely believe with all my heart that God placed this particular book in your hands so at the end of your life, you will have no regrets. There will be no "would've, should've, could'ves," and no guilt that you could have done more to move His Kingdom forward.

I find that many believers who love God and love Jesus, do not necessarily love God's churches. It is a sad but true commentary. There are multiple reasons this occurs. Many of those people have been hurt or offended in church and have decided, enough is enough. Can you imagine the number of hurt people in our cities who, at one time, were active members serving in the local church. Now they have no association with any church whatsoever. Most of us know someone that fits into that category. If truth be told, we know more than we care to admit. Heartbreaking! There are those who have been disenfranchised and confused by all the religion that has crept into churches over the last 2000 years. What do I mean by this?

CHRISTIANITY BECOMES RELIGIOUS WHEN THE BELIEVER PUTS A CHECK MARK IN THE "WENT TO CHURCH" BOX ON SUNDAY AND FOCUSES MORE ON SYSTEMS, RITUALS, TRADITIONS, PROCESSES, AND DUTY INSTEAD OF DEVELOPING A HEALTHY, PASSIONATE RELATIONSHIP WITH <u>JESUS CHRIST.</u>

There are also people who have just merely slipped out of the habit of going to church, most likely blaming a busy lifestyle for their sabbatical. It is more probable that their comfort zone made it easy to *not* go to church, whereas in church, you are definitely *out* of your comfort zone. In order to maximize your time in *The Build*, it is not enough that you love the Kingdom, or even that you want to be a servant or leader in the Kingdom, you must see the Church and the many local churches the way the Father and Jesus sees them. I believe the desire of our hearts should always be to view and value things and people in the same way as the Father, Jesus, and the Holy Spirit. That is something I believe we can all agree upon. How should we see God's churches? Why are they so important? Does going to church really even matter? I absolutely love these questions. For years, I have studied church/revival history and consider myself a bit of a historian. When I read about the lives of the great men and women of God who have impacted and changed the world, I am so inspired to pay a greater price to move deeper in the things of God. The sole purpose is to impact His Kingdom in a greater way. I have studied the Welsh Revival with Evan Roberts, Alexander Dowie and Zion, Illinois, William Seymore and the Azuza Street Revival, John G. Lake, Smith Wigglesworth, Charles Parham and the outpouring of the Holy Spirit in Topeka Kansas, Aimee Semple McPherson and the Foursquare Movement, F.F Bosworth, the Voice of Healing Revival, William Branham, Oral Roberts, Jack Coe, A.A. Allen, Gordan Lindsay, Billy Graham, Kenneth E. Hagin, Lester Sumrall, T.L. Osborn, Katherine Kuhlman, and so many more. These people are my heroes. They influenced me to want to give my life for the Gospel. The thing is, they are all dead. Praise God, they are all in Heaven. Great men and women of God live and die. These heroes of faith, come into the world and will all eventually leave this world, but the true Church and God's local churches around the world continue to flourish century after century.

GOD'S TRUE CHURCH AND HIS LOCAL CHURCHES AROUND THE WORLD HAVE CONSISTENTLY ACCOMPLISHED THE KINGDOM BUILDING FOR THE LAST 2000 YEARS.

Where would the world be today, where would you be today, if it was not for the work of the Church over the last 2000 years? As believers, we do not have the luxury of loving God, loving Jesus, and loving the Kingdom without loving His Churches. I used this analogy in *The Move*, our first book. It makes my point so well that I will restate it again. I love my children with my whole heart. If someone approached me and stated how much they love me and appreciated me, but then quickly informed me they could not tolerate my kids. We would have a problem, a big problem! There would be no relationship between me and that person. Why? To truly love me, you should also love and value what is most precious to me, and that is most definitely, my children.

TO LOVE GOD IS TO ALSO LOVE WHAT IS MOST PRECIOUS TO HIM AND THAT IS HIS CHURCH AND HIS MANY LOCAL CHURCHES AROUND THE WORLD.

I can comprehend a believer having no desire to be a part of a specific church. Whatever the reason may be, pray for those churches, walk in love, forgive if a wrong occurred, so that you can stay free of unforgivness. Then, ask the Holy Spirit to guide you to a church where you love and connect with the vision of the church. A place you can envision yourself growing in the Word, worshipping deeper, fellowshipping with others, serving, becoming a Kingdom leader, and **BUILDING THE KINGDOM**. No church is perfect, just as no believer is perfect, but we need each other. We are stronger together.

The reason I wrote *The Build*, again with full discloser, is so you can transition from believer to servant, from servant to leader and give your life to…

1. Leaving the Church bigger and better than how you found it.

2. Leaving the Church stronger for the next generation.

3. Knowing that as a Kingdom leader, you moved the Kingdom forward.

In this book, *The Build*, you will be given numerous tools in which to build the Kingdom, God's churches, and a great life. *The Build* is filled with stories, revelation, and in Chapter 2, you will find the beginning of 203 nuggets (I call them Builds) that I pray will BUILD you and help you BUILD others. Here is a heads up. This book is not super spiritual! *The Build* from start to finish was written to deliver the most amount of truth with the least amount of words possible.

The Build is practical, simple, clear, applicable, rememberable, precise, quotable, and full of a passionate love for the Kingdom, the Church, and for leaders that I hope and pray is contagious.

Let's Build
Phillip Baker

CHAPTER 1

Breaking Containment

Years ago, two words were spoken to me that shook me from the inside out. These two words embodied everything I wanted to see happen in the lives of people, in my life and especially in God's churches. Those two words were:

Breaking Containment

Personally, I hate ruts, plateaus, and that awful feeling of being stuck. The thought that a year could pass and I would be in the exact same place as I was the previous year is absolutely unacceptable to me. I truly believe in my heart that the people, pastors, and Kingdom leaders that are reading this book feel the same way. Like me, you are always reaching to learn, expand and grow.

In order to break containment, we first must understand that satan is the master of containment. He desires to contain our knowledge, our perception, our success, our finances, our physical condition, our calling, our ministry, our relationship with the Holy Spirit and the Word, our relationships, our vision, our anointing, our influence, our church, and ultimately - the Kingdom. We see this containment clearly in Acts 4:15-17. The Pharisees were being used greatly by the devil, said, (concerning the disciples and the word of Jesus' death, burial, and resurrection) *"But that it spread no further among the people, let us straitly threaten them."* Do you plainly see satan's plan for us and everything God has called us to do? Satan does not want us to **spread further**. His desire is to contain, repress, stifle, subdue, control and restrain us. It is what he has been doing effectively for over 2000 years.

SATAN DOES NOT WANT US TO SPREAD FURTHER

Here is a great question. What does this containment of the enemy look like? This was the question that I asked The Holy Spirit. How can we expect to overcome containment if we do not recognize the form it takes in our life? As I began to pray and seek answers, the Holy Spirit began to show me something in my heart. I pray that you know the Holy Spirit still speaks to us and reveals God's plan in a way we can understand. I began to see anchors. Imagine a boat floating steady on the water, being held in place, unable to move freely, because deep below the surface, there is an anchor at work. Imagine now, a life, a ministry, or a church, floating in place throughout months and years, restrained from moving forward (doing what a boat was created to do) because anchors are diligently working behind the scenes to ensure it remains contained. The Holy Spirit began to show me three anchors that keep us from advancing, keep us in a rut, and contain us on the plateaus of life. These anchors have been in existence for a long time and have held so many people, pastors, churches, and Kingdom leaders in the position of being STUCK.

The Anchor of "Deserve"

The first instrument of containment I saw was, the <u>Anchor of Deserve.</u> Many people believe that whatever they have and wherever they are in life is ultimately what they deserve to have and where they deserve to be. These thoughts are solidified by the enemy whispering a lie into the ears of believers. The lie is simply, you should be grateful for where you are and what you have because so many people around the world would love to be in your position. Yes, we should be immensely grateful, but, at the same time, have a Kingdom desire to always be growing and taking new ground. One of the reasons for people being so defined by the realm of deserve is because we have more of a revelation of what we have done wrong as opposed to a revelation of what we have done right. People have more of a revelation of their weakness before they accepted Jesus as their Lord and Savior than they have of their potential after coming into the Kingdom. We must have a real understanding that Jesus Christ did not come to accomplish all He did at Calvary, so that we could get what we deserve. He came so we could reach out with our faith and receive amazing grace (which is more than just a song). Grace is getting what we do not deserve. We do not deserve salvation, but God's grace. We do not deserve healing, but God's grace. We do not deserve the Holy Spirit, but God's grace. We do not deserve to be a Kingdom leader, but God's grace.

The Anchor of "Ignorance"

The second anchor I saw was, the <u>Anchor of Ignorance</u>. Here is the thing, we do not know what we do not know. The definition of ignorance is, "the lack of knowledge or information." When you do not know something, it opens the door to being deceived. Deceived is a bad place to be, because when you are deceived, you do not know you are deceived, because you are deceived. You may need to read that again. During the Dark Ages, most people were ignorant concerning the Kingdom because there was such a void of wisdom and revelation. The written Word of God was hidden away by religion and kept out of the hands of the true church. It is hard to imagine a time when every household did not have access to a Bible. Here we are today, with an abundance of the Word at our disposal with the simple click of a button, and yet so many people are still ignorant of the Kingdom. During one of my trips to Africa, I observed a muslim forum where people were posing questions to an Imam (the person who leads prayers in a mosque). One of the muslims asked the Imam, "Why do you think so many muslims are leaving the faith and becoming Christians?" I was completely convinced that at any moment, the crowd was about to stone that person, but the Imam gave an answer that I never forgot. He said, "So many muslims are leaving Islam because they get lured away by the blessings of Christianity and they are ignorant of Islamic teaching." I thought this was an interesting response, because often times I wonder how many believers are not thriving in their faith and life because they are also ignorant of the Kingdom of God and how it operates? In order to be a Kingdom leader that will see growth in everything we put our hands to, we must be humble enough to continue to be teachable, continue to learn, and willingly embrace change. No one has arrived yet, but praise God, we have left. No doubt you are walking in the knowledge you have, but surely you understand there is always, always, always more. The wisdom of God is infinite. The heart of a Kingdom leader is to be consistently less ignorant today than we were yesterday.

The Anchor of our "Comfort Zone"

The third instrument of containment I saw was the <u>Anchor of our Comfort Zone</u>. As soon as a human being comes out of the womb, they intently embark on the mission to build their comfort zone. People want to be comfortable in the church and out of the church. I have come to the belief that the greatest threat against The Church is not so much the devil himself, but in his ability to contrive and induce us to a place where we are more loyal to our comfort zone than we are passionate about building the Kingdom. I will never forget a prophetic word the Holy Spirit gave me years ago…

You will become comfortable in the realm of risk Or you will risk everything by living in the realm of comfort.

We all could learn so much from the story of Zacchaeus in Luke chapter 19. That grown man climbed a tree and got out on a limb. That could not have been his comfort zone. The result was Jesus went home with him and his life was forever changed. His act of risk is still being talked about today. The effects of that risk is still changing lives. Everything you want in life, all the growth and success will require that you climb some trees and get out on some limbs. In order to do this, you must bust free your comfort zone, because nothing extraordinary happens in your comfort zone. Learn from Jesus. He had to leave the comfort zone of the carpenter's life in order to be the Lord and Savior of the world. Kingdom leaders are more loyal to the Kingdom than they are to their comfort zone and in the days ahead, if we will step out of our comfort zone, we will begin to see containment break.

As I said before, satan is the master of containment and he has built a war machine to keep us stuck, in a rut, on a plateau, and CONTAINED so that we spread no further. I believe I know the very moment this particular war machine of containment cranked up its engine.

Mark 16:15 Jesus says, "Go into all the world and preach the Gospel to every creature."

There it is! Jesus said something He had never said before. Up until that point, the Hebrew had only ever heard, STAY in Israel. Now, Jesus is saying, go to the world with the Gospel. Do you think satan heard this? Of course he heard this! He could not allow believers that were filled with the Holy Spirit, armed with the mighty name of Jesus, and with the knowledge and ability to live by faith as well as walk in love to go into all the world unhindered. It is the exact same situation we have today. Satan does not want Kingdom leaders, God's churches, and ministries infiltrating the world and successfully building the Kingdom.

Do you want to build the Kingdom? Do you want to matter? Do you want to make a difference? Do you want to do your part? I believe you do, or you would not have continued reading this far into this book. Turn the page and the beginning of 203 nuggets (I call them, Builds) will be yours in which to ponder and meditate. These Builds were written to encourage, challenge, and teach you how to **BREAK CONTAINMENT.** These BUILDS were written to help you **BUILD** your life, ministry, family, church, and ultimately the Kingdom. Are you ready?

Let's build.
Phillip Baker

CHAPTER 2

LEADERSHIP BUILDS

When I have the privilege and honor of standing before leaders in the local church, I always begin by asking this question, "Do you have some wet wipes with you? We are about to get our hands dirty?" There is a huge difference between looking at an aesthetically beautiful car vs. popping the hood and carefully examining the engine. You must understand my heart. I love the local church so much. When we "pop the hood" on the church and understand what makes the church run, we will get our hands dirty. In "popping the hood" we will endeavor to understand and answer these questions. Why are so many churches not growing? Why is the average church in America typically around 60 people? Why churches have been built by a few people doing a lot, instead of everyone doing something? Kingdom leaders should not be defined by their title, but by their heart for Jesus, their heart for people, and their heart to grow in wisdom. Years ago, there was a movie called "Field of Dreams." Great movie! In the movie, the main character hears a voice to build a baseball field in the middle of nowhere on farmland that should be used for crops to save the farm. The voice exclaimed, "If you build it, they will come." The church laid claim to that idea and ran with it. The church mistakenly thought that if they built a building, a pastor preached in the pulpit, then people would surely come. I believe we know, it is not that simple. As Kingdom leaders, we must be open to change. How does that look? We must begin to learn some things we never knew. We must be willing to hear some things we have never heard and see some things we have never seen. Let's build.

Build #1 - All About Building

Building His Kingdom, Building His leaders! I cannot think of a better way to spend one's life, than doing both. What the precise impact a person can make concerning this endeavor is unknown, but to live your life with full assurance you left the Kingdom and leaders BETTER, STRONGER, and BLESSED is something we should all aspire too. I will absolutely spend the rest of my life passionately doing both. Join me.

Build #2 - The "Not A"

In order to be a Kingdom leader, you must know that Jesus Christ is *THE* way, not *A* way. Jesus Christ is *THE* truth, not *A* truth. Jesus Christ is *THE* light, not *A* light. That has to be settled in your heart, because in the days ahead, this truth will be tested in every church, every family, every believer, and in every Kingdom leader. This issue must be settled in your heart and mind now. This is the foundational truth for any leader that desires to build the Kingdom.

Build #3 - Kingdom and Church

The anointing builds the Kingdom, leadership builds the Church! This declaration is at the very core of both PBM and *The Build*. I love the anointing and I love leadership. I believe with all my heart we can have excellence in both that will result in making a huge impact on the Kingdom of God. By the way, I do not believe it should be 50/50, but instead, 100/100.

Build #4 - The Anointing Builds The Kingdom

The anointing builds the Kingdom! Jesus Christ provided for us through His death, burial, and resurrection, the person of the Holy Spirit and the power of God. With the power of the Holy Spirit we can build the Kingdom throughout the earth knowing we have the victory and we have received authority over satan, sin, sickness, and poverty. This is what "The anointing builds the Kingdom" means to me.

Build #5 - Right Growth

The anointing plus little leadership equals little growth of a church. Big leadership plus a little anointing equals big numerical growth in a church. Big leadership plus big anointing equals right growth where a church is growing *BECAUSE* the Kingdom is being built. When the anointing and leadership is a priority, growth that pleases God will happen. We do not desire one or the other, we need *BOTH*. Consider this, just because souls are being won into the Kingdom, does not necessarily translate to the church growing numerically. On the other hand, Churches that put people into seats does not always equate to souls which are being won into the Kingdom. Again, we want *BOTH*. We can have both, however it will require work.

Build #6 - Strong In Both

There are churches that are anointing heavy and leadership light. They build the Kingdom, but the majority of those churches have not grown numerically, in a long time. On the other hand, there are churches that are anointing light and leadership heavy that do not make a major impact on the Kingdom, but are running thousands. I have zero desire to judge specific churches. I just want to be a part of raising churches that are strong in both the anointing and leadership. Those churches are changing a community, a city and a region.

Build #7 - Many Sides To A Mountain

The subject of leadership is like Mt. Everest. That mountain has many sides and features to it. Leadership does as well. We can spend a lifetime talking about leadership, studying leadership and never understand all that leadership encompasses. The main objective is that we embrace the amazing subject of leadership, enjoy the journey, continue learning and do not get offended, and together let us make a difference in our family, church, community and in The Kingdom of God.

Build #8 - Never Been Taught

Here is one of the main reasons I wrote this book! The Build was written for all the Bible school graduates and ANYONE (Bible school graduate or not), who has a desire to build The Kingdom, pastor churches, be youth and children's pastors, or praise and worship leaders. These wonderful people with their heart in the right place know

The Word, but have never been taught the very important leadership side of ministry. How many people enter ministry knowing doctrine, but have not been taught leadership? These are dedicated people who want to make a difference. They know The Word but also need to know how to motivate, inspire and bring people together. The Build is for you.

Build #9 - Why So Important

This is why leadership is so important! When you do not understand principles of leadership, the easiest thing to do is to reproduce what you have experienced in life. Let me give you just one example. If you grew up in a home that lived pay check to pay check, you will repeat that example if you do not learn a different way. Try this! Take a look at your life and determine if it is a reflection of the world in which you grew up. Is your life defined by the circumstances and events of your younger years, and the people who impacted your life? Those experiences, when negative, will demand you learn and adjust and reconstruct what you have seen to negate that influence. When those experiences have been positive, there are most likely people you need to track down and thank.

Build #10 - Out Of The Cage

When I was a teenager, I was part of a youth group that consisted of approximately 15 people. When I became a youth pastor, I had a youth group with around 15 teens. Let me say it one more time. When you do not understand leadership, you will reproduce and recreate what you have seen. Why? Because it is comfortable and it is what you know Your past experiences can be a cage in which you must break free. Please know, it will not happen by accident. You must acquire knowledge and expand your thought process beyond your current set of skills. Learning requires that you hear some things you have never heard, see some things you have never seen, and go some places you have never gone. Breakthrough will not be found in your comfort zone.

Build #11 - Hence Leadership

When you do not understand leadership, you will reproduce what you have seen in life. The average church in America is approximately 60 people. What that means is many pastors were raised in churches of 60 people. So, the easiest, most comfortable thing for these pastors to do is pastor a church of approximately 60 people, because they have seen it, they know what is required. Many times pastors brought up in small churches, pastor small churches, and pastors that grew up in big churches, pastor big churches. It does not have to be this way, hence leadership!

Build #12 - Poverty, Marriage, and Health

When you do not understand leadership, you will reproduce what you have seen in life. This applies to more than just church. People brought up poor, will find it easier to stay poor. People brought up seeing a dysfunctional marriage will find it easier to have a dysfunctional marriage. People brought up in a home with unhealthy eating habits will find it easier to keep those bad habits even at the detriment of their health. I hope you see how important it is to make the connection of your past experiences and influences and what is currently taking place in your life. When you are able to connect the two, your journey to break free has begun.

Build #13 - Time To Step Up

Stewardship believes that when you are faithful over little, God makes you faithful over much. (Luke 16:10) This statement is what leadership is all about. You cannot separate stewardship from leadership. Leaders are ultimately stewards of God's people and Gods Kingdom. God is looking for us to step up and be His STEWARDS in the earth. Remember, when you are a good steward, more responsibility is coming. I hope that excites you, not scares you.

Build #14 - Yes, You Are

We have heard it said often, "Leadership is influence!" Absolutely! Everyone has some measure of influence. In other words, somebody is watching us. We all matter. We are all impacting the life of someone, either positively or negatively. I do not want to hear, "I am not a leader!" Yes, you are! I am! I do not want to hear, "What I do, does not matter!" Yes, it does! Everyone is either a good leader or a bad one. Everyone is either influencing people around them to make good decisions or bad decisions. One day, we will give account for that influence and whether or not we were a good steward with it.

Build #15 - The Pursuit of Excellence

Leadership is all about the word, EXCELLENCE! Leadership is the pursuit of excellence in every area in which we have influence. Imagine the excellence we will experience in Heaven. It will be unimaginable! Jesus said, we are to pray that it would be on earth as it is in Heaven. (Matthew 6:9-13) Part of that prayer is telling us that we should pray that the excellence of Heaven would also be seen in our life, business and church. We must endeavor to bring this excellence from Heaven on everything in which we set our hands.

Build #16 - Disney World

Years ago, I took the family to Disney World! I was amazed at the standard of excellence everywhere I looked. While I was there, I never saw one dead flower or anything that was broke. Believe me, I was looking! I did not see trash on the ground, even though there were people everywhere. The customer service was amazing. Everything and everyone was on time. Disney World is the closest that man can come to Heaven, but I believe it we be a dump compared to the majesty of Heaven. Be a Kingdom Leader that pursues excellence in all things. Those that choose excellence on earth, will feel right at home in Heaven.

Build #17 - There Is A Plan

Do you want to get out of debt? Do you want to lose weight? Do you want your business to grow? Do you want your church/ministry to grow? Pray! During your time of prayer, ask the Holy Spirit for a PLAN! Write that plan down, implement the plan, and ask for power to execute the plan. The Holy Spirit has a plan for anything you want to see grow. Most believers want to pray, but want nothing to do with the word, PLAN. Be A Kingdom Leader who prays, gets a plan, and sees breakthrough in all things. Yes, it is that simple!

Build #18 - A Serious Thing

In Acts the 6th chapter, leaders were raised up in the church because people were being neglected. Today, I believe we would all agree that there are many people being neglected due to a shortage of servants and leaders. In the end, seven people were chosen to lead. Think about it, everyone was eligible, but not everyone qualified. Leading in God's Kingdom is a serious thing! Being responsible for the lives of others should be taken seriously! Take your influence as serious as the seven people did in the early church.

Build #19 - The Anointing To Lead

In Acts the 6th chapter, leaders were elevated to meet the needs of the people. Seven people were chosen. They were brought before The Apostles, and hands were laid upon them during a time of prayer. When hands were laid upon them, an anointing came upon their life to serve and to lead. There is an anointing for leadership in The Kingdom! Seek after that anointing. You will need it to do what God has called you to do.

Build #20 - Ready For GREATLY

In Acts the 6th chapter, Leaders were advanced in the Church to meet the needs of the people. When this was done, The Word increased, and the number of the disciples multiplied in Jerusalem GREATLY! Are you ready to see

GREATLY in your life, business, and church? Raise up leaders! Invest in leaders! Spend time with leaders! Remember, God did not raise these leaders, The Apostles did. WE must raise leaders to see GREATLY!

CHAPTER 3

SERVANT LEADERSHIP

You may not already know, but in 1994 through 2003, I had the honor of being the Director of an incredible Bible school in Columbus, Texas, called Texas Bible Institute. I learned and grew immensely during that wonderful season of my life. One day in particular, something happened that I would never forget. I was asked to gather a handful of students to pick up all the rocks that had been scattered by the construction of a new road that had recently been established. That day, we were expecting a children's camp. As you can imagine, rocks, several hundred children, and glass do not go well together. I presumed there were no students who would willingly volunteer to spend their entire afternoon picking up rocks. Would you? As I thought about the issue, an idea came to me. I went into the classroom where hundreds of students were being dismissed from class to go to lunch. I informed the students that I had placed several buckets just across the street. They were instructed to walk out the doors upon dismissal and gather 5 rocks each and put them in a bucket. As their fearless leader, I would collect 6. Within 5 minutes, the job was done! With the help of everyone, the task was easy and quickly accomplished. This is how the church should operate. For so many years, I have endeavored to raise up "five rock churches." Not suggesting you find 5 things to do in the church, however insinuate everyone must do their part. It means that the church would be full *of participators and not just spectators. It should go without saying (but I will say it anyway) that your place in the church is not your seat, but your place of service. The Father has called us to be servants. He has called up to do **our** part. He has called us to be a "five rock leader." In order for you and I to be a "five rock leader," we must have a servant's heart. Let's build.*

Build #21 What About You?

The journey of leadership always begins by embracing the role of a servant. Jesus Christ was a servant. The disciples were servants. The people in the early church were servants. The Apostle Paul was a servant. The people of Heaven are servants. Angels are servants. What about you? Have you been a servant in the Kingdom and God's churches? For those that can answer, YES, thank you for all you have done and are doing. For those that chose to answer honestly, NO, it is never to late to begin to serve. Your gifts and talents are valuable. Time to get started.

Build #22 A New Rule

What is a servant? Simple! A servant is someone who serves, assists, helps and supports because they have the heart of a servant. A servant is not someone who just goes to church. That would be equivalent to saying, all those that are in a kitchen are chefs. New rule! Those that do not serve, do not get to call themselves servants. That unfortunately means, they are not like Jesus, the disciples, the early church, everyone in Heaven, or the angels.

Build #23 The Battle Cry

The battle cry of a servant in the Kingdom of God and God's churches is, "Many hands make a light load!" The Kingdom and God's churches have been built by a few people doing the majority of the work instead of by everyone doing something. No wonder people burnout. They are carrying loads that are simply too heavy for one person to maintain. The weight of the Kingdom must be redistributed throughout the entire Body of Christ. It is time for everyone to do their part.

Build #24 Waiting Around?

A true servant does not wait for the important position to come along. The servant does not wait for someone to ask them to help. The servant sees a need and meets it. In the process of serving wherever and whoever, promotion takes place, trust is built, doors open, opportunities come along. What if you are not waiting on God, but in reality, God is waiting on you? Go meet with your pastor or church leadership and ask them where the church requires some help. You will see a huge smile come upon their face. To be honest, you might also see a look of shock, because they may have never had that question asked to them before.

Build #25 Get in the Funnel

Some of the best advice I have ever received was from Paul Troquille, a dear friend. It went something like this. Ministry is like a funnel. When you begin, you start at the top, the widest part of the funnel. There are so many things to do, so many choices, so may experiences. As you serve, you begin to work your way down the funnel to the small end or your specific life calling. Let me say it again! You start on the big end, doing what is necessary and as time goes on, you work your way down the funnel to the small end which is more defined, precise, clear-cut, definite. The most important part is to leap into the funnel. Begin to serve wherever there is a need.

Build #26 Got Started Yet?

Many do not know that I started in ministry by serving in Magnolia, Arkansas. For four years I was the youth and children's pastor at Magnolia Christian Center. I also cleaned the church, took care of the sign outside, ran a bus route, and coached a little league team. It was a great season of my life. I learned a great deal and developed as a young minister. Everyone has to start somewhere! So glad I got started all those years ago. Have you got started yet?

Build #27 Titles, Positions, and Authority

While attending RHEMA Bible Training Center in 1989, Brother Kenneth Hagin Sr. said something so powerful that it has stuck with me even to this day. He was addressing several hundred very green, very eager, soon to be Bible school graduates. It went something like this, "When you get back to your church, don't go looking for titles, positions, and authority, go home and serve. Go home and be a minister. Go home and assist your pastor wherever there is a need. Go home and be a blessing." Never forgot it. I believe the heart of God is for us to serve, minister, and be a blessing.

Build #28 Supernatural Leaders

In the Kingdom, and in the Church, you will find an abundance of "you get it" or "Someone else will do it" when we need the inclination of "I've got it." Find a need and fill it. That does not mean you take over someone else's job. There are plenty of areas to serve. Don't be a spectator, be a participator. Be a servant, not a customer. When something needs to be done, have the attitude, "I've got it." Imagine what the Kingdom would look like today if everyone had an "I've got it" attitude.

Build #29 Willy Wonka and the Chocolate Factory

Do you remember the movie, "Willy Wonka and the Chocolate Factory?" Do you remember the Oompa Loompas that did everything in the factory? They smiled, sang, had fun and did all the work. **There are NO Oompa Loompas in the Kingdom and Church.** Servants are serving in the Kingdom all over the world every day. Servants are serving in every church before services, during services, and after services every week and every day in between. Everything that is being done to build the Kingdom is being done by servants. Are you one of those servants?

Build #30 I'll Pray About It

When a need is presented in God's Kingdom and churches, people love to say, "I'll pray about". Let me translate that statement for you. It simply means "NO". It means, "I do not want to". When we do not want to serve, we turn super spiritual. I believe the most amazing way to show how super spiritual we truly are is by having a servant's heart!

Build #31 Not My Anointing

When a need arises in the Kingdom or church, people love to say, "That's not my anointing". Here we go again. Allow me to translate. It simply means, "I do not like them". Here is an example. "We need help with the children". People respond with, "That's not my anointing." Translation! "I do not like children". It is amazing how people can over spiritualize things when they do not want to help or it is not in their comfort zone. Remember, the anointing we have dwelling in our spirit is ultimately to be used to bless people.

Build #32 Too Many Excuses

Young people cannot serve because they are too young. Adults cannot serve because they are too busy. The elderly cannot serve because they are too old. Wow! What are we going to do? How will the Kingdom be built? Everyone has a reason or excuse why someone else will have to do what needs to be done in His Kingdom and churches. Time to drop all the excuses and SERVE.

Build #33 Grace is Given

For 10 years, I had the honor of serving at Texas Bible Institute in Columbus, Texas. It was a great season in my life. During that season, I was asked to perform many duties I did not feel equipped or trained to undertake. I succeeded because I truly believed that if authority asked you to do a task, the Father would give you the grace to complete it. I love grace! Become a servant and you will find the grace to complete an assignment. That grace is only found in your obedience and willingness to be used.

Build #34 The Good Stuff

When authority asks you to do something, and you endeavor to do it with a great attitude, God will give you the GRACE to do. In that GRACE is creativity, the anointing, and blessings! The good stuff is in the GRACE that comes from obedience. Creativity, the anointing, and blessings are found in the life of believers who have a servant's heart.

Build #35 Hands to the Plow

When Elijah found Elisha, Elisha was plowing a field. In other words, when the call of God found Elisha, he was busy doing something. He was working, not sitting under a tree waiting to be found by the call. To summarize, put your hands to the plow in the local church and the call of God will find you. Elisha's life was forever changed when he was found by the call and so will yours.

Build #36 Kingdom Synergy

The power of synergy is amazing! Synergy is 1+1=3 not 1+1=2. In other words, the more people you have serving, multiplies production. There will be an incredible synergy when we get to Heaven, therefore there should be an incredible synergy in families and churches! Be a part of Kingdom synergy. Find a place and a people to serve along side and it will be amazing what will be accomplished. You will be able to be a part of something and see the Kingdom built in a way you could not have done on your on.

Build #37 Culture is Everywhere

"Culture is the characteristics and knowledge of a particular group of people, defined by everything". (Webster's Dictionary) Everywhere you go in the world, you will find culture. Every country has a different culture. Some countries are loud, some are quiet. Some countries are confrontational, and some are laid back. Some countries are very religious, and some are secular. Some countries are very much about community, and some are very isolated. Every church has a culture and that culture determines if they will be successful building the Kingdom.

Build #38 Customer Culture

Every church should have a particular culture. Before I tell you what that culture should be, let me tell you what that culture actually is, most of the time. Churches have a customer culture. People walk into church the way we walk into restaurants. Today, we walk into a restaurant and go into critique mode. We like this, and we do not like that. That may be fine for a restaurant, but do not bring that into the church. We are not in church to critique as customers, but we are there to serve as servants.

Build #39 Customer Equals Pharisee

I want to give you another word for customer. How about Pharisee? From the moment Jesus Christ came on the scene, they were critiquing everything He did. They liked this, but did not like that. They liked that He healed a man, but He should not have done it on the sabbath. They liked that He ate with people, but He ate with the wrong people. The Pharisees absolutely missed what God was doing in the earth and we will too, if we do not get the customer culture out of God's churches.

Build #40 The Servant Culture

Every church and family should have a servant culture. The church should be a place where everyone helps, puts their hands to the plow, pitches in, asks "what needs to be done or what can I do to help?" "I've got it," and SERVES! When you find a church with a servant culture, you will find a church where the vision is thriving, God is pouring out His presence, and revival is in reach. Everything a church can be, begins with having a servant's culture.

Build 41 The Great Revival

All my life I have been hearing about a great revival that is coming. Every church in which I travel is believing for revival. Where do you think God will pour out revival? Will He pour it out on a customer culture? Will He pour it out on a servant culture? Once again, we always think we are waiting on God, when truly He is waiting on us. By the way, when revival does hit in churches, how many servants will be needed to sustain all the activity taking place in every classroom throughout the church, the lobby, the sanctuary, in the parking lot, and don't forget about the bathrooms?

Build #42 Built On Revelation

In order to develop a servant culture in the Kingdom and church, we must build it from God's Word. You cannot build that culture from using need, guilt, and duty. People must receive a revelation from God's Word concerning servanthood. They must see that when they serve, they are following the path of Jesus, the disciples, the early church, the Apostle Paul, the people of Heaven, and God's angels. This servant culture must be built on revelation. A servant culture must be built from the inside out, from the heart first, then in our actions. Identity determines function. Never forget that.

Build #43 All Generations

A servant culture must be built into all generations. Young people today want to serve, not just be lectured to. They want to do something. Why can't we let them share, greet, and sing? Why can't we get together and brainstorm all the ways that young people can be a part of the team instead of expecting them to sit down, shut up, and just listen? We must release ownership into all generations. No one is too old or young to serve. Maybe, if we will do this, we will have a church one day where the majority serves as opposed to where a few serve.

Build #44 River of Appreciation

In every church and family there should be a river of appreciation that flows continually. Where there is a servant culture, you will always find honor and gratitude for those who are participating in the vision on any level.

Never let anyone go unthanked for anything! Never take anyone for granted. Never become too familiar with someone who is serving day in and day out. Never believe someone if they say, "Everything I do, I do for Jesus, and I do not need to be thanked". No one is so super spiritual that they do not need to be appreciated for all they do for others. In the Parable of the ten lepers, Jesus *noticed* that only one came back to say thank you.

Build #45 So Much Baggage

One of the reasons it is hard to build a servant culture in the church is because people carry baggage from past experiences that they have had in other churches. So many people have been hurt while serving elsewhere, that they do not want to serve at all. All this negative baggage is why the love of God must be preached so that people can become free from fear and unforgiveness. The love of God must be taught in order for people to come into a greater love for God and for people. The love of God must be preached so that we do not hurt those that God has sent to our churches to receive LIFE! There is NO servant culture without a revelation of the love of God.

CHAPTER 4

SUPERNATURAL LEADERS

Many years ago, I ministered to a group of pastors on Tana Island in the South Pacific Ocean. It was such an honor to spend time with them, encourage them, and share many of the things that are in this book with these wonderful Pastors who are building God's Kingdom on a small island that most people do not even know exists. In between the daytime sessions and the night crusade I found a couple of hours to snorkel in the beautiful waters. I was told where to enter the water and then to walk out about 30 yards where there would be a drop off. I slowly, with shoes on, walked out on a rocky surface to the drop off. Upon arriving at the drop off, I was blown away by what I saw. With water up to my knees, I looked over and saw a drop that would be the equivalent of looking off the top of a building. It was kind of scary! I had a decision to make. Was I going to jump in? Was I going to stay in the shallows or jump into the deep? What about you? Are you going to jump in? Will you stay in the shallows or jump into the deep? Will you be a natural leader or a supernatural leader? One more thing, I did jump in. It was a decision I will never forget or regret. That day I saw coral reef, fish of every color, and water as clear as crystal. It never would have happened, if I didn't jump. God's Kingdom is supernatural and His Kingdom leaders are supernatural leaders. Let's build.

Build #46 Supernatural Leaders

We need more supernatural leaders in the Kingdom! We need leaders who are not easily offended, are on time, have character, know how to follow as well as lead, are emotionally mature, and most of all, are led by the Spirit, not their flesh. The Church has enough natural leaders. The Kingdom needs you to be a supernatural one because Jesus is coming back soon and we have work to do.

Build #47 Feed Yourself

Can you imagine having to feed an adult that was completely capable of feeding themselves? No way! With this thought in mind, a supernatural leader feeds themselves the incredible Word of God. What we get from church, what we get from pastors, should be the icing on the cupcake, not the cupcake. Get in your Word more than ever in the days ahead. Supernatural leaders read the Word, study the Word, and meditate in the Word. It is a top priority in their life.

Build #48 A Great Follower

A supernatural leader knows they must be a great follower before they can lead and impact people. Can you imagine walking into a Navy recruitment office and asking for the admiral's application? The officer would think you were trying to make a joke. In the Kingdom, we must follow before we lead, we must be able to follow an order before we give one, and we must learn serving before we can step into ruling.

Build #49 Will not be Offended

I WILL NOT BE OFFENDED! This should be every supernatural leaders declaration. In the Kingdom, ministry, and church you will get many opportunities to be offended. People will be mean and insensitive. Many people will not appreciate what you do. You will be taken for granted. It will happen! What are you going to do? You and I are going to walk in love, not be offended, and build His Kingdom and His leaders. That's what you are going to do.

Build #50 "Buttonology"

Do you know someone that pushes your buttons? Here is a question for you. What gives you the right to have buttons? Jesus was buttonless. Satan was continually coming at Jesus, through people, to push His buttons. Satan failed every time because Jesus did not have any buttons. We, like Jesus, are to be buttonless, as supernatural leaders. Over the years, as I have taught this idea, and have declared that I have a degree in buttonology. I am a buttonologist. When I declare that, people usually laugh and that's fine but this is a subject I take very seriously. We must get rid of our "buttons" and do something great in the Kingdom. Yes, I know I made up some words.

Build #51 What's Your Message?

What subject in the Word are you passionate about? What do you like to study in the Bible? What would you teach if you were standing in front of a group of people? A supernatural leader has a message that is dear to their heart. It is so important that you develop that message. In that message, you will find the anointing, favor, grace, and strength when times are hard. It will be in the sharing and the living of that message that you will make the greatest impact in the lives of people.

Build #52 Here is Mine. What's Yours?

When I was young I was right in the middle of a horrible church split and saw a great number of people hurt by the split and I witnessed a church hurt by it. The people who were hurt the most were the children of those involved. From these events, I found my message on the love of God. I have studied that subject more than any other. I have preached on the subject more than any other. It is at the core of everything I preach and do and is the central message of my life. What's yours? A supernatural leader knows.

Build #53 First Class Character

Character is, who you are in the dark. Character is, what you would do if you knew for certain no one would ever find out. When the electricity goes out in a city, what happens? There is always looting, isn't there? The dark did not make them steal, it just revealed their true character. Character is something that a supernatural leader must possess. With first class character, you can make an amazing impact on the Kingdom. Leaders whose character fail, will bring a reproach on the gospel and leave hurt people in their wake.

Build #54 Fresh Oil

In the Old Testament, priests were to keep oil in the lamps. When the lamp would run low of oil, the flame would be ugly and the odor would be bad because the wick was burning. We are to keep fresh oil in our lamps. When we do not keep a fresh anointing in our heart, our wick begins to burn and we put off an ugly flame and a bad odor. As supernatural leaders, it is our responsibility to have a fresh oil. (Psalms 92:10) Get in the Word, worship, and spend time with the Holy Spirit.

Build #55 River of Creativity

We need a river of creativity to flow through our churches and our supernatural leaders. Do we really want the world to be more creative than the Kingdom of God in the earth? We should not be going to the world for ideas, the world should be coming to the church. We serve the CREATOR, not them. We must get out of our dull, lazy, comfort zone, and creatively express the magnificence of the Kingdom! Creativity, flow In Jesus Name!

Build #56 The Idea Rules

In order for a river of creativity to flow in our churches, ideas must flow freely in the hearts and minds of supernatural leaders. Ideas must be celebrated. Here are two guidelines to make sure this process doesn't blow up in our face. #1. Do not attach emotion to your ideas. People tend to feel that if their idea is rejected, then that means they personally are being rejected and they get their feelings hurt. We do not have time for this kind of emotional immaturity. #2. Do not attach **"GOD SAID"** onto your idea. When you place **"GOD SAID"** onto your idea, you have no choice but to be offended if the pastor does not approve and celebrate your idea. At this point, you have no choice but to believe that he didn't think you heard from God. Here is what you do, give your idea and trust God then trust the pastor or leader. If they do not like your idea, wait a few moments and give them another.

Build #57 Hat Dynamics

No doubt your pastor wears many hats. When you are with them, what hat are they wearing? When I began in ministry, I worked under a great man. There were times he was my boss, times he was my pastor, and there were times he was my friend. It was not his job to inform me which hat he was wearing, it was my responsibility to know the difference. To be a supernatural leader you will have to understand "Hat Dynamics." Leaders that do not, will find themselves offended, confused, and eventually out of ministry.

Build #58 Have a Great Day

For 10 years, I was the director of a tremendous Bible school in Texas. This Bible school was for ages 17-25. Needless to say, there was much drama, and it was my job to handle issues. In ministry, there will always be drama, because it involves people. To have longevity as a leader, you will have to decide that you are going to have a great day and there is not anything anyone can do about it. For a supernatural leader, a great day is a choice, not a feeling based upon the circumstances of the day or the mistakes of others.

Build #59 Always Excited

In ministry, in church, there will always be events, campaigns, and a focus for a certain season. A supernatural leader will be excited about each season. What if I am really not excited, though? Here is what you do! Put a smile on your face, get some energy in your words, and make a decision to get excited. You not being excited is not an option. Because if you are not excited, the people you serve will not be excited. A leader leads by example. Welcome to the world of leadership. Isn't that exciting?

Build #60 The Big Picture

A pastor of any local church has many more responsibilities than the project in which you are presently focused. He has much on his mind. It is easy to get so focused on your responsibilities that you forget there is a big picture. Be a supernatural leader who sees the big picture. It will give you a GRACE to work with your pastor and other leaders in the church. Supernatural leaders who have the ability to see the big picture are a great blessing to their pastor.

Build #61 The Happy Life

Laura and I decided years ago that we would NEVER be more excited than we are right now. We have maxed out HAPPY! I wasn't happier last year. I will not be happier next year. Let me ask you this. Are you born again? Does Jesus live in your heart? Will you spend eternity in Heaven? What else do we need to be happy? Joy may come and go with the events and circumstances of life, but a supernatural leader has made the decision to be happy based upon what is in them, and not what is going on around them.

Build #62 Pay the Debt

Who impacted your life for the Kingdom? Who believed in you? Who was there for you? Who prayed for you? Who discipled you? Who taught you? Who inspired you? The people that are coming to your mind right now have something in common. They were supernatural leaders, and we MUST become supernatural leaders to pay that debt forward. We must impact others the way our life was impacted.

Build #63 No Egg Shells

Is there someone you know, that you must walk on egg shells around? You know what I'm talking about. We all know someone like this. You must tread lightly around "you know who" because they might get upset, mad, and or easily offended. Be a supernatural leader and NEVER be this person. No one should have to walk on egg shells, watch every word they say or tip toe around you because you are moody or emotionally mature. It should never be your pastor, your family or any people in general. Get the broom and sweep away any possible egg shells that are at your feet.

Build #64 High EQ

Everyone is familiar with the IQ (Intelligence Quotient). It is so beneficial to have a high IQ, but I believe it is even more important to have a high EQ (Emotional Quotient). To be a supernatural leader you must have a high EQ! You must be emotionally strong. You do not have the luxury of being a roller coster emotionally, up one minute, down the next, happy one day and angry the next. When people see you, they should not be wondering if you are going to be mad, glad, or sad. Think about this. How many people have been hurt by leaders with a low EQ? The answer is too many to count and more than likely, YOU!

Build #65 The Thank You's

Over the years, I have had the joy of seeking out supernatural leaders who invested and influenced my life to say, "**THANK YOU**" I will humbly tell you that since going into ministry in 1990, I have had many people reach out to me and say, "**THANK YOU**" for impacting their life. We do not spend a lifetime building the Kingdom and building leaders for the "thank you" but, when you receive sincere appreciation, it is life changing and something you will never forget. Let this Build remind you again that people ARE always watching and being impacted by your life. One of the reasons I wrote this book was so that you may receive many sincere, "**Thank you's**" throughout your life.

CHAPTER 5

VISION LEADERSHIP

In South Houston, in the city of La Marque, there is a massive greyhound dog track. People come from all over to watch the dogs run, as well as gamble on which one will win. What makes the dogs run? Do you think the dogs care about which one is the fastest? No! The reason the dogs run with all of their energy, is because they are chasing a rabbit. The rabbit is not real, the rabbit is on a pole that has the ability to move around the track faster than the dogs, but the dogs know none of that. They are oblivious to the pole. The dogs are chasing the rabbit! What are you chasing? What is your rabbit? Let's back up a moment. What if there was no rabbit? What would the dogs do? How would they act? For those of you that have ever owned a dog, you know. The dogs would do three things. They would begin to wander around, they would commence to smelling each other, and they would become aware of all the people and instinctively yearn for the people to pet them. When people do not have vision in their life, when they do not have a rabbit, they do the same things as the dogs. They begin to wander through life with no purpose or plan. They begin to put their nose where it does not belong by always involving themselves in the gossip of those around them. They begin to desire the attention of others, and no matter how much attention they get, it is never enough. God created us for VISION. He created us to be a vision leader.

One of the favorite words of a Kingdom leader is VISION. Let's build.

The Build #66 Live VISION

I have the opportunity to speak to numerous people in churches and it is always a joy to meet God's people. What I have noticed in all my years of ministry is that most people are only capable of talking about the past, not the future. I find it to be a common thread. Their life is defined by where they have been, not where they are going. What is even more sad is that most recollections that are relived and retold, tend to be the bad memories and events, as opposed to good memories. Live VISION, not memories!

The Build #67 Visionaries

One of my favorite subjects to teach is vision! We were created by the Father to operate in the realm of vision. Life stalls and begins to fall apart when we step out of that realm. You are at your very best when you are in that realm. When you read the Word you will see that the great men and women of faith lived vision far more than they lived memories. Today I am declaring that you and I are **VISIONARIES.** Declare it now, "**I AM A VISIONARY**".

The Build #68 Alexander the Great

Alexander the Great did something brilliant when driving his army into foreign lands. Every morning, a group of soldiers would leave the camp early and plant a pole miles ahead in the direction the army was marching. The army knew there was a pole, and when they reached the pole, they would be allowed to stop to rest for the night and eat. I imagine they were on constant look out for that pole. The army had a vision! What is your vision? What is your pole? Where are your eyes? Are your eyes focused on where you are going or where you have been? Do not let an unsaved, heathen King out vision you!

The Build #69 The Front Windshield

There is a reason the front windshield in a car is big and the rear view mirror is small. We are to stare out the front windshield and only briefly glance at the rearview mirror. It is the same in life. Stare at where you are going and glance at where you have been. For those who do the opposite, you will become acquainted with accidents. Live vision, focus on where you are going, and occasionally glance back at where you have been. For those of you who execute front windshield living, you will have a great life.

The Build #70 Chase The Rabbit

At a greyhound dog track the dogs run because they are chasing the rabbit! In other words, because of their vision, they are running. Habakkuk 2:2 tells us to write the vision, and make it plain upon tables, that he may RUN that reads it. Here are two great questions. How can you write the vision down if you do not have one? What else will produce the "run" in our life without vision? God has called us to run towards our goals and vision, not wander aimlessly through the storms and circumstances of life.

The Build #71 Eyes on the House

Two boys in a snowy field made a bet with each other concerning who could walk a straighter line in the snow back to their house. One boy focused on his feet, heel toe, heel toe, while the other boy kept his head up and eyes on the house. Whose path do you imagine would be straighter? That's right, the boy who kept his eyes on the house. What are your eyes fixed upon? What is the vision that is keeping your path straight? Take your eyes off your feet, off your circumstances, lift your head, lift your eyes, and focus on what's ahead.

The Build #72 The Vision Leader

The vision leader is fueled by passion and conviction. This enables them to have a sense of ownership concerning their assignment. They do not serve because they have to, but because they get to. The vision leader's heart is to take their assignment and maximize its potential. When passion, conviction, and ownership come together, you will find excellence, anointing, and increase.

The Build #73 The Duty Leaders

The duty leader is polar opposite to the vision leader. First of all, the duty leader is not bad, because a duty leader is better than no leader at all. The duty leader serves out of duty, not passion. The duty leader serves because they feel obligated to, not because they get too. Many times when someone does something out of duty, they think they are doing the church a favor. Let me be strong with this thought, **NO ONE** has ever done their church a favor. God does us a favor by allowing us to serve in **HIS CHURCH**. Be a vision leader and operate out of passion.

The Build #74 Develop the Art

Vision is the art of seeing something no one else sees. When I was a teenager, I saw a traveling ministry in my future. There were many people that did not see what I saw. As you can imagine, there were people who did not believe in my vision. Get ready! There will be people who will not believe in your vision. What will you do? Will you give up the dream in your heart? Since 2003, I have been in over 50 churches a year throughout the world. If I am living **VISION**, so can you.

The Build #75 Got Lack

Wherever there is lack, there is a lack of vision. Make a list of all the areas where lack is present in your life. Take a look at your list. These are areas where there is a lack of vision in your life. Do you have a vision for your finances, health, marriage, home, business, ministry, and life? When you bring the many areas of your life into vision, you will see provision. Let me say that again, where there is vision, you will soon see provision. Live a vision life!

The Build #76 A Vision Issue

You can have an average product and a great vision and be very successful. On the opposite side of the spectrum, you can have a great product and an inferior vision and fail. What does it say that churches have the Word of God, yet so many close their doors everyday? Is it the Word's fault? No! Many times it is a vision issue. What about you? Think about all you have in Christ. Are you seeing the success you want to see? Is it the Word's fault or is it a vision issue?

The Build #77 Honey Oat Bread

Subway is one of the largest franchises in the world. Why? They made a decision to corner the bread market. What is the first question they ask when you walk in? Their vision was to win customers by providing a choice of wonderful breads. What is your favorite bread at Subway? Come on, you know you have one. They do sandwiches well. They do bread great! Find out what God has equipped you to do great and start doing it. When you do, you will be living a vision life. Don't let Subway out vision you.

The Build #78 McDonald's are Everywhere

Did you know that McDonald's is not just in the food business? They are in the kid business. Their vision, for a very long time, has been to create a place and a menu that kids would desire and beg their parents to take them. They do many things good. They do food good. They do kids great! Find out what God has equipped you to do great and begin doing it. When you do, you will be living a vision life. Don't let McDonald's out vision you.

The Build #79 Your Favorite Sonic Drink?

Sonic made a decision years ago that their vision would be to corner a drink market. They have more varieties and combinations than anyone else, happy hour, and of course, "sonic ice." They do food good, but they do drinks great! You have a favorite sonic drink? Come on and admit it! Learn from Sonic! Do everything as good as you can, but do one thing great! When you do, you are living a vision life. Don't let Sonic out vision you.

The Build #80 Master of Something

We are not meant to be a "jack of all trades and master of none" person. There is a little restaurant in Leona, Texas that makes the most mouth watering, incredible steaks. Seriously, it is on my "top 3 steaks ever eaten list." People drive from all over to enjoy them. They have a very small menu. They are open only Thursday - Saturday at night for just a few hours. There is always a line outside waiting for the doors to open. They do numerous things good. They do ONE thing great. Find out what God has equipped you to do great and get busy. When you do, you are living a vision life. Don't let Leona's out vision you.

The Build #81 Studio 54

Back in the late 70's, there was a famous nightclub called Studio 54. Yes, I know it was the epicenter of hedonism. It became the most famous nightclub in the history of all nightclubs. The reason for its incredible success was simply because the owners had a very clear and defined vision for the club. That vision, by the way was very demonic. That nightclub was demonic. That's the power of VISION! Vision is a principle that works, even in the world. Don't let someone's demonic vision exceed your Kingdom vision.

The Build #82 What's Different?

It is not what you do the *same* as others that sets you apart, it is what you do *differently*. When we began PBM in 2003, what made us stand out and be different was the leadership training we provided for God's churches. That diversity opened many doors. There is something God has called you to do that is distinct from everyone else. Discover your uniqueness and commit to it with excellence, and watch life will fall into place. When you embrace what you do different, you are living a vision life.

The Build #83 God for a Day

Let's just say for a moment that you are God for a day. On this day, you are scouring the earth for a church in which to pour out your presence. Do you pour our your power on the church operating out of VISION or the church doing everything out of DUTY? The answer is simple for you and for the Father. The **VISION CHURCH** will receive the **OUTPOURING!** The vision church will obtain the **BLESSINGS!** The vision church will acquire what the DUTY church will not.

The Build #84 Favor Poured Out

Favor is getting escorted to the front of the line. Favor is getting somewhere twice as fast with less effort. Favor is when you pull off of a dirt road in life and hit a smooth paved highway. You must be aware that this kind of favor follows passion. Someone who is operating out of VISION instead of just DUTY, will always have more passion about the Kingdom and Kingdom work. Let's recap. Vision first, followed by passion, and finally FAVOR! Do you want the Favor of God poured out on your life? Live a VISION Life.

The Build #85 Vision Draws People

In general, people desire to be part of something bigger than themselves. This is exactly the atmosphere that vision creates. This atmosphere can be created in the church, youth department, praise and worship team, and every department in a church. This atmosphere can be created in a business also. When this happens, people will become eager to be a part of what is happening. People will drive long distances. People will wait in long lines. People will pay any price. Vision attracts people. Your vision will attract people.

The Build #86 Vision Draws Help

People want to help leaders who are passionate and have a conviction about what they are doing. People want to connect with vision leaders. It is not true of duty leaders who use guilt to manipulate people to sign up and serve. People will ask the vision leader *TO* help, instead of the duty leader asking *FOR* help. Here is a great question, if someone does not have anyone helping them or desiring to help them, are they operating out of vision or duty?

The Build #87 Vision and Character

When a person is operating out of vision, you will find greater character. Remember, character is who you are when no one is looking. Character is who you are in the dark. A vision leader who is passionate about what they do, would never do anything to jeopardize the success of their Kingdom assignment. They would never do anything to hurt the people they serve. They would never do anything which might bring a reproach on the gospel.

The Build #88 Vision And Excellence

When a leader is operating out of vision instead of duty, you will find a higher level of excellence. Excellence is doing the best you can, with what you have. Many times, the person who serves out of duty, believes that whatever they are doing is just fine and appreciated because at least they are doing something. Of course, we should appreciate whenever someone does something, but Jesus gave us His best and I believe we should give the Kingdom our best.

The Build #89 Here is your Vision

"Brother Phillip, what is the vision for my life?" I am so glad you asked. Your vision is to be who God has called you to be, do what God has called you to do, and help others find out and do what God has called them to do. Can you imagine how strong the Kingdom of God would be if everyone said YES to their vision? Let us learn from the ultimate vision leader, Jesus Christ. He fulfilled His vision and helped so many others discover theirs.

The Build #90 Very Sad

During my many years in full-time ministry, I have had only a handful of people (that is being generous), sit me down and sincerely inquire about the vision for my life, what I was passionate about, what I thought I was created to do. How about you? I would bet, it is a small number. I have had many people go on and on and on about their vision. When you sit someone down and begin to ask questions about the vision for their life, you will create a moment that they will remember for a long time. Do for others what very few people did for you.

CHAPTER 6

Leadership Attributes

Tanzania, Africa is a beautiful country. I have had the honor of ministering there on numerous occasions. Over the many trips, God has taught me amazing things and every time I go, I come back with a richer anointing. On this one particular occasion, He showed me something that will stay with me throughout the rest of my life. We were on our way up the mountain to teach in the Bible school in Arusha. We were driving very, very slow, simply because we were traversing the worst road in the history of the world. People were literally walking faster than we were driving! I was in the back seat, and I noticed a little girl standing some distance ahead on the side of the road staring off in the distance without an expression on her face. The closer I got to her, the more I could not take my eyes off of her. As the car slowly drove right next to her, and we became face to face, her face was still expressionless. All of a sudden, we were staring at each other eye to eye, and I simply gave her a big smile. What do you think she did? That's right, she gave me a big smile right back. Why did she smile? I believe it was because I truly saw HER. There are so many people in the world that want and need someone to simply see them, to notice them. They live their life feeling invisible. I do not want anyone feeling invisible or insignificant, especially in God's churches. Since that moment, everywhere I go, I endeavor to communicate with a big smile to people that I see them. Amazingly enough, every country I visit, when I look people directly in the eye and smile they ALWAYS smile back. Kingdom leaders have a smile that lights people up. I promise, Jesus Christ had one of those smiles. Kingdom leaders have other attributes as well. These characteristics are as straightforward and impacting as a simple smile. Let's build.

The Build #91 Firm Handshake

Kingdom leaders have strong, positive body language. Body language informs people you are confident. It tells people if you are emotionally mature. It notifies them if you are a strong person or a weak person. Walk tall with your head up. Sit up straight and lean forward a little bit when listening and talking. By all means, please, have a firm handshake. Very few people will take you seriously if you offer them a weak, wimpy, soft, handshake. Body language speaks volumes about you well before you ever open your mouth.

The Build #92 Be Teachable

Kingdom leaders are teachable. When you are teachable, it shows that you are eager to learn. Being teachable requires that you listen. Being teachable requires that you pay attention to your surroundings and learn from the success and failures of others. Being teachable requires that you appreciate what you know, but are even more interested in what you do not know.

The Build #93 Be on Time

Kingdom leaders are on time. Being on time shows your priorities are right. Over the years, I have heard the reason people are late is because they are on "southern time," "northern time," "Africa time," "Mexico time," "Island time," and the list goes on and on. The bottom line is people are ON TIME for movies, concerts and free meals. I think you get my point. People are on time for what is important to them. It is a priority and discipline issue. Leaders should always be on time (15 minutes early) because what is more important than the Kingdom?

The Build #94 Smile BIG

Kingdom leaders have a smile on their face. Our smile is proof of positive Kingdom living. Let your light shine and smile. Your smile tells people so much about you. Your smile comforts, soothes and reassures people they are welcome to the group or room. Your smile in an incredible way to introduce them to Jesus, who by the way, is going to blow us all away with His smile.

The Build #95 What Happened to Manners?

Kingdom leaders have manners. Manners show you have respect for others. Manners show you respect people in general. Leaders that say, "thank you," "you're welcome," "Yes Sir," "No Sir," "Yes Ma'am," "No Ma'am," and "please". Manners are open doors for those approaching. It is not a "southern thing," it is common courtesy. We all would reap respect if we would make a habit out of showing respect. Here is something to ponder. One of the greatest gifts we can give children are manners. When we do, we are preparing them to be successful in life.

The Build #96 A Strong Work Ethic!

Kingdom leaders have a strong work ethic. Your work ethic will be noticed by everyone you serve. It does not take long for people to decide if you are lazy or committed to that which you believe. When you have a strong, personal work ethic, people will know you are a leader who walks the walk, not just talks the talk. When people see your standards are high and you work hard, they will raise their standards and work hard as well.

The Build #97 Be Sincere

Kingdom leaders are sincere people. The person who is sincere has an honest soul. Sincere in the Greek means, "without wax". It was back in Bible days that you wanted to purchase a garment that was without wax. In other words, you wanted a garment that was held together by thread, not wax. You wanted a garment that was sincere and not fake. You wanted a garment that would hold together when the hot sun of the day would come beating down. Today, we need leaders, more than ever before, who are sincere and that will not fall apart when the heat is applied.

The Build #98 Be Faithful

Kingdom leaders are faithful. Being faithful tells the world you are predictable and consistent. The Kingdom of God is in grave need of people who are devoted, committed, trustworthy, unswerving and reliable. The opposite of what I just described are those whose lives resemble a roller coaster in their emotions. There is enough erratic and chaotic behavior in the world, therefore, we need leaders who are the opposite. We need leaders who are faithful, day in and day out, rain or shine, and in good times or bad.

The Build #99 Just Listen

Kingdom leaders listen. Listening is a learned behavior that many do not possess. When you listen, you show you have the much needed ability to control your mouth. Do you know someone who does not have that ability? Sure you do. These people always control the conversation. Even when you are talking, you know they are not truly listening, but instead, they are thinking about what they want to say. When you listen you are showing people you honestly care about them and the situation they are going through. When you actively listen, you are able to discern, by the Holy Spirit, if and what you can say that will precisely inspire, aid, console or build up the person in who you are sharing your heart.

The Build #100 Be Thankful

Kingdom leaders are thankful When you are thankful, you show people you are not spoiled. When you are thankful, you show people you are not entitled. When you are thankful, you show people you are not so familiar with blessings that you take them for granted. Speaking of spoiled and entitled, don't you hate buying something for that kid in the family that is picky, spoiled and not thankful? No matter how much you toil over just the right gift, they will quickly open it, look at it, then throw it to the side without regard or acknowledgment and move on to the next gift. Don't be that kid in the Kingdom, church, or life in general.

The Build #101 Be a Giver

Kingdom leaders are givers. When you are known as a giver, you have proven to the world that you are not selfish. Neither the sinner nor the saint enjoys being around selfish people. They both will go out of their way to avoid being involved with anything that a selfish leader is doing. Another reason leaders must be givers is because every leader in God's churches desires for those they serve to be givers. We must live by example. You cannot expect someone to be something you are not.

The Build 102 Do You Tithe?

Kingdom leaders are **Tithers**. Let me say it again! Leaders are **TITHERS**! Everything a leader does, and who they do it for, and what they do it with, is most likely provided by the tithes of the people from the church. There would be NO church or opportunities to serve, if there was no tithe. How in the world can a person in a church flourish in leadership which is directly linked to the tithe and not tithe themselves?

The Build #103 What Happened to *Kind*?

Kingdom leaders are full of God's love. When you are full of love, the outward expression is kindness. What happened to just being nice? What happened to being polite? I know in the Kingdom, hard decisions must be made often, but I do believe we can still be productive without being rude, obnoxious, or just plain mean. Do not tell me you cannot be a great achiever in the Kingdom and not be nice, kind, and polite. I believe you can.

The Build #104 RIGHT Relationships

Kingdom leaders have positive, RIGHT relationships. When you are in relationship with people that increase you, it shows you walk in wisdom. Do your relationships bring out the best in you? Do your relationships encourage you to always do the right thing? I have been saying it for years, "Relationships build the Kingdom!" No one reading this BUILD has enough God, Kingdom, right relationships to do all God has called them to do. Examine the relationships in your life and decide which ones are wisdom and which ones are not.

The Build #105 Right Place, Right, Time

Kingdom leaders are at the right place at the right time doing the right thing. This style of life indicates you are Holy Spirit led. When you are not Spirit led, you will be at the wrong place, at the wrong time, doing the wrong thing. We have all been there before and things did not work out so well, did they? Listen to the Holy Spirit, let Him guide you and life will be so much better and a whole lot more fun.

The Build #106 24/7 Greeter

Kingdom leaders greet people and make them feel welcome. Greeting visitors and church members show that people are a high priority for you. I think it is great that churches have a greeting ministry. The possible problem, though, is that in some cases, people that are not involved with the greeters team assume they do not have to greet people. Can we just settle this train of thought once and for all? For all you leaders out there, you are on that team *in* church and *out* of church, because people are a high priority for you. Right?

The Build #107 A Leader's Eye?

Kingdom leaders have a leader's eye. When you have a leader's eye, you show you also have a spirit of excellence. Is trash on the ground? Does a light need to be turned off? Does a toilet need to be flushed? Does a picture need to be straightened? The leader's eye is possessed by someone who has developed an attention for detail. This form of leader wants the excellence of Heaven to be manifested in the church, ministry, and surroundings where they serve.

The Build #108 Say I'm Sorry

Kingdom leaders say they are sorry. When you apologize for a mistake, it allows people to see that pride does not control you. When you make a mistake, and we all do, do not justify or minimize your mistake in order to save face. Look the person in the eye and sincerely apologize and let them know that you will endeavor not to do it again. You may be thinking to yourself, "if they will apologize, then I will apologize!" *You* doing the right thing has NOTHING to do with whether or not they will do the right thing. Owning your mistakes is not weakness. It comes from a place of strength, security and humility. Do the right thing.

The Build #109 Righteous Indignation

Kingdom leaders should have righteous indignation. When someone is harming the Kingdom, God's churches, or God's people, your response with a righteous anger demonstrates your love and desire to protect. Your anger is directed at the offense, not the person. What is the difference between anger and righteous indignation? Jesus got mad when they were defiling the temple or keeping the children from Him. He never became angry at anything done to Him.

The Build #110 Restaurant Manners

Kingdom leaders behave themselves in restaurants. What? That's correct. Leaders behave themselves in restaurants. Do you order the most expensive item on the menu when you are not paying? Do you get up and go to the restroom when the ticket arrives at the table? Do you eat faster than everyone and finish first? Are you so focused on the food that you forget you are there to build a relationship? Are you kind and respectful to the waiter? Do you act disrespectful or curt when something is not up to your standard? Are you a good tipper? It is amazing how the everyday task of eating with someone at a restaurant can acquaint you with the true character of a person. Represent the Kingdom when you walk into a restaurant as if you were walking into your church.

CHAPTER 7

Precision Leadership

Have you ever experienced back pain? I sure have! Years ago, I had a problem in my lower back. I had been receiving adjustments by a chiropractor for several months and even though it had relieved some of the pain, the discomfort was always present. One day, I had had enough! I walked into the office of my doctor and informed him that we were starting from scratch. I told him I would lay on the table and begin to move around. Every time I felt pain, I would point to it. So, that is exactly what I did. I laid down on the table and began to move and point, move and point, and move and point. My doctor, who is amazing, just leaned against the wall and intently watched my every move. When I had completed this task, he said, "You know, it might be that your sacrum is off." He began to examine my body and discovered that my sacrum or tailbone was a little crooked. He made an adjustment to his usual treatment protocol. At that moment, the adjustment did not feel much different than usual, but I hoped there had been a breakthrough. I went home that day and although my back was not perfect, it was better. I returned in two days and told him to do the exact same adjustment as before. He did. I went home and my back showed continued improvement. Again, two days later, I returned and again he repeated the new adjustment. My back was feeling better than it had in a very long time. Three adjustment and I was good! Listen carefully, the reason I received a breakthrough was simply because I communicated, with precision, my situation. So many times, we do not receive what we are seeking because we are vague in our communication, instead of being explicit, detailed and precise. Kingdom leaders must communicate with precision. When we do, the outcome is growth, success, and breakthrough! Let's build.

The Build #111 Embrace Precision

PRECISION - "A measurement, performance, or communication that can be used as the highest standard." (Webster's Dictionary) We must move away from vague communication in the Kingdom, churches, and business. Embrace communication that is clear, precise, accurate, exact, direct, and specific. When I think about the word, PRECISION, I think of a clock that always has the right time. Our communication should be as precise as any timepiece.

The Build #112 Four Amazing Words

Four incredible aspects of leadership are inspiration, motivation, expectation, and appreciation. These four amazing words, that rhyme by the way, must be communicated in the Kingdom and churches with precision. Sad to say, most of the time, these 4 words that should define what we do are communicated in a very vague way. I hate vague and so should every precision leader.

The Build #113 Vague is Everywhere

There is so much frustration that we experience in our life that comes directly from vague communication. How often are husbands and wives frustrated in a marriage because they are communicating what they need and want vaguely? How many parents and children are frustrated because they are communicating expectations vaguely? How many Pastors, leaders, and members are frustrated because "vague" describes most of their communication? It is time to get PRECISE.

The Build #114 Where are we Going?

We must be precise if we want people in the Kingdom and churches to experience inspiration. Inspiration is all about where we are going. Being in a car on the way to vacation is far better than being in that same car on the way back. Inspiration in a church comes when the vision (where we are going) is communicated with precision. When people in a church are not engaged or involved, it is a reflection of a poorly communicated vision or NO vision at all.

The Build #115 Abstract Paintings

In order to communicate a vision precisely, the vision itself must be clear. In Africa, there is an amazing museum with many different kinds of art. My personal favorite is photography while my least favorite is abstract painting. The vision must be as clear as a photograph and not as vague as an abstract painting. When a vision is abstract, it leaves room for interpretation by the viewer. When the vision is clear, it will be easier to communicate it in a way which inspires creative ideas and action.

The Build #116 Vision & Provision

The vision of a church or ministry must be communicated with precision. When the vision is vague, and communicated vaguely, it will be forgettable. When the vision is communicated precisely, there will be two things that will always follow; 1. The people will be inspired to action. 2. There will be provision. When people are not actively engaged with the project or there is a lack of provision, it is not necessarily an attack of the enemy or apathetic people. Make sure the vision has been communicated in a straightforward, positive manner if you are not seeing things moving forward.

The Build #117 True Results

"Write the vision, and make it plain upon tables, that he may run that readeth it. Habakkuk 2.2" The precision leader writes the vision down as simple and as clearly as possible and communicates it precisely. The result over time will be people that will be inspired to build the Kingdom and there will be more than enough provision to do everything that God has put on their heart.

The Build #118 True Motivation

In order for people to experience true motivation, we must communicate "WHY" with great precision. People are not motivated to do anything if they do not know why they are doing what is being asked of them. Too many times we assume they know, but far too often, they do not. We tell children to do things and they want to know "WHY?". Our response is, "Because I said so!" That might half-way work with children, but it does not work with adults. That is simply, poor leadership skills.

The Build #119 Boundless Energy

There is no such thing as lazy people, there are just people who are not properly motivated. As leaders we must find what motivates those to whom we are assigned. Explaining to people why they are doing something, is a good start. When the "why" is vague, you will be ignored. When the "why" is communicated with precision, there will be energy, creative ideas, inspiration and insight. It is time for boundless energy in the Kingdom and church, and using precision to communicate "WHY" is a great key.

The Build #120 Are There Expectations?

In order to be an effective leader, you must learn to communicate expectations with precision. What do you expect from people? What do you expect out of yourself? Is there accountability attached to those expectations? Sometimes, in a church or ministry, we are so grateful to have someone serving that we place no expectations upon them. We place no requirements upon people serving. There are no standards or accountability and then we are surprised and disappointed when the fruit is minimal.

The Build #121 We Have Work to do

In the secular world, there are expectations that come with a job. In most cases, you are provided with job requirements. When those expectations are not lived up to, you might find yourself out of a job. I do not believe the church should act like the world, but Jesus is coming back soon and we have work to do. We need leaders that embrace expectations and are challenged by them, not leaders who avoid or are even offended by them. What is going on in the Kingdom and God's churches is so important and we need people who will bear fruit consistently.

The Build #122 Rise Up

Someone may say, "When you place expectations upon leaders and servants they may quit leading and serving." People may quit, but at least we are not operating out of fear that they will. Someone else may say, "What if they quit because they do not live up to those expectations?" I truly believe those that are serving want to do a good job. They want to make a difference and would embrace boundaries and expectations. I believe we are wise enough to make sure the expectations placed on others are reasonable and not impossible. This is what I say, "What if we place expectations on people and they rise up and do incredible things to build the Kingdom of God and His churches?"

The Build #123 Increase

When a precision leader communicates expectations with great clarity there will be increase in the Kingdom, in churches, in departments, and in businesses. When these expectations are communicated poorly or not at all, you will always get a repeat of the last year. I hope you have the desire to always be appreciative of what has been accomplished in the previous year, but at the same time, desire increase with all of your heart for next year. I believe "this year" should always be greater then "last year." Increase is always God's will for the Kingdom, churches, and ministries.

The Build #124 Never Unappreciated

A precision leader absolutely loves to appreciate all the people he has the honor to serve. He appreciates his pastors. He appreciates all people. He appreciates people's giftings, passions, and their journey in life. He appreciates moms, dads, business people, teachers, and all those who are faithful. No one EVER feels unappreciated around a precision leader.

The Build #125 All In

We should never quit looking for creative ways to communicate appreciation with precision.When appreciation is communicated vaguely or not at all, you will eventually have people that will disconnect. When appreciation is communicated with precision, people will feel connected, valued, important to the vision. They will feel linked and connected to where the ministry is going. They will be ALL IN. We need people to be ALL IN.

The Build #126 Front of the Church

I believe it is great when we call someone to the front of the church and pray for them as they are embarking on a mission trip. Let's think about something. If we only ever call someone up to pray for their upcoming mission trip, what does that tell everyone? I would never want someone to think that the only people who are special are those who are doing ministry/missions work. Let's celebrate and pray for those getting a new job, getting married, opening a business, graduating school, and the list goes on and on. Find ways to celebrate people.

The Build #127 Atmosphere of Honor

I believe precision leaders work very hard to create an atmosphere of honor in the church or wherever they are serving. A dear pastor friend took several of his members to a church that had been in revival for many years. They loved the service, but were even more impressed by the hospitality, honor, and appreciation they experienced from those they encountered in the lobby. They met precision leaders who had created an atmosphere of honor in the lobby and throughout the church departments. They did it and we can too.

The #Build 128 36, 20, 1

In Romans the 16th chapter, the Apostle Paul mentions 36 people by name that blessed his life. He greeted or saluted these wonderful friends of his 20 times. In that chapter, he tells them to MARK those that cause division only 1 time. I think if we spent more energy saluting and greeting people and building strong relationships with them, maybe we would not have to do as much MARKING. The Apostle Paul was a precision leader.

The Build #129 The LIE

Precision leaders never believe the lie. There will always be people who will say they do not need to be appreciated, because knowing Jesus sees it all is enough for them. No one is so super spiritual that they do not need a sincere thank you for all they do. Let's make sure we do not take people for granted, become familiar with their faithfulness, assuming they know we appreciate their service to the Kingdom and the church.

The Build #130 See People

When a leader communicates appreciation vaguely, people feel insignificant. It is one thing for people to feel insignificant in the world, but they should never feel it in the House of God. When a precision leader communicates appreciation clearly, you are letting people know you SEE them. In Africa I saw a little girl and gave her a big smile, when I did she gave me a smile back that I will never forget. Why? I SAW her. People desire to be SEEN.

CHAPTER 8

KINGDOM CHURCHES

Years ago, I heard a story that captured my heart. Over the years, I have told this story to many congregations. I thought it might be the perfect story to introduce these Builds to God's wonderful churches. One day, two men were hunting in the woods when they encountered a huge hole in the ground. It was like some sort of endless pit. So one man says to the other, "I wonder how deep this hole is?" They tossed rocks in and listened ... nothing. Being intrigued, they began looking around for something larger to throw into the hole. One man spied an old transmission hiding in the bushes. They decided they would throw the transmission in the hole and surely they would hear it hit bottom. They inched the heavy transmission towards the hole and dropped it in. The men were looking down the hole when all of the sudden they hear a noise in the woods. Then out of no where a goat came running out of the woods and dives, head first into the hole. As they were pondering what they just saw, a voice behind them said, "Hello gentlemen!" The man who had walked up was the owner of the land. He was a nice gentlemen who was just checking on things. After they chatted for a moment, the gentlemen asked the two men if they had seen his goat in the area. The men paused for a moment then said, "Sir, we hate to tell you this, but right before you walked up, your goat ran out of the woods and jumped head first into this deep hole." The gentlemen then said, "That's impossible, my goat is tied to that transmission right over there". This story is a perfect picture relating the importance of what and who you are connected. That goat was connected to something that took him where he did not want to go. We are living in the last days. We are living in perilous times. It is so important that you are connected to the right things and the right people. In the days ahead, become connected to the Kingdom more than ever before. Kingdom leaders are connected to the Kingdom, one of the Father's local churches, and the vision of the pastor. Let's build.

The Build #131 The Answer

Jesus is the answer for every person. The Holy Spirit is the answer for the Church. The Church is the answer for the world. In the days ahead, we cannot back down from these beliefs. They are absolutes. One more thing, with the Church being the answer for the world, how important are the leaders in those churches? Be one of those leaders! Be an answer for the answer.

The Build #132 One Incredible Road

Jesus is *THE* Answer for every person. He is not "*AN* answer," He is *THE* answer. There are not many roads to Heaven. There is one incredible road to Heaven and to the Father and that is through His Son, Jesus Christ. Leaders in God's Kingdom and churches must stand on this truth and not bend to all the pressure that the world is applying. By the way, the pressure will only get worse.

The Build #133 He Has The Answer

The Holy Spirit is the answer for the Church. There was no church until the Holy Ghost fell on the day of Pentecost. Every question that can be asked concerning the Church, the Holy Spirit can answer. The heart of a Kingdom leader is to have a greater relationship with the Holy Spirit so they can be a greater blessing to the Church. Holy Spirit, reveal yourself to me, in me, and through me.

The Build 134 The True Church

The Church is the Answer for the world. Great men and women of God come and go. It is the cycle of life. The heroes of faith live and die, but the Church just keeps moving forward. Over the last 2000 years, it is the true Church that has gotten the job done. Be a big part of the Church! The Father needs you to be a servant, a leader, and a big blessing in His Church.

The Build #135 Grows and Thrives

"I like my church just the way it is!" I rebuke "just the way it is" in Jesus' Name. The person who says this might as well say they do not care if people go to hell. We have work to do. Praise God for all the seats that are full, but what about the ones that are empty? We must operate with a sense of urgency in these last days. I pray that your church grows and thrives and you have to deal with the gall of someone sitting in your seat on a Sunday or a Wednesday. Imagine the horror.

The Build #136 A Faith Church

I was on the phone recently with a dear friend who had been through a lot that year. He had doctors tell him some things no one ever wants to hear. He has come through it and has a wonderful testimony now, praise God! He said something that really stuck with me when we spoke. He was so grateful that when he was in the middle of it all, he attended a FAITH CHURCH. This church stood with him in faith not just sympathy. Do you attend a faith church?

The Build #137 A Plan From Heaven

Many churches pray this prayer. "We call them in from the North, South, East, West." Well, in order to see the Kingdom and churches grow we must to do more than just pray. Prayer alone does not produce growth. One of the great purposes of prayer is to receive a plan from heaven. The purpose of prayer is also to receive power from heaven to fulfill that plan. As leaders in God's Churches, let's get in His presence and receive a plan and power. We will then see things grow and thrive.

The Build #138 Scream at the Wheat

As I just mentioned in the above build, many churches pray this prayer. "We call them in from the North, South, East, and West!" Matthew 9:38 tells us to pray that God would send laborers into the harvest. It does not say, pray that the harvest would come to the laborers. Stand in a barn and scream at the wheat to get in the barn and see how that works out for you. As Kingdom leaders we must first pray, get a plan, receive power for the plan, and then go to the harvest and bring it in. At the same time, if you want to call the people in from the North, South, East, and West, then go for it.

The Build #139 Power of Expectation

By the time Jesus would get to a city, the expectation of the people would be at frenzy level. The stories of the miracles that had taken place in the ministry of Jesus had spread to the area like wildfire and the people's faith would be incredibly stirred. They were ready and expecting to receive THEIR miracle. What if we took some time on the way to church and ignited our expectation. I believe we would see so many more miracles.

The Build #140 Don't Leave, GO

Faith doesn't leave, it goes. Abraham did not just leave his country, he was going to a land that God would show him. (Genesis 12:1) Laura and I did not leave Texas Bible Institute in 2003, we were going to Dickinson, Texas, to birth Phillip Baker Ministries. Make sure when you are leaving a city, job, or church that you just do not leave. Faith is always advancing to a new assignment, promotion, or a greater season. When people leave, many times it is because they are hurt and that is not how you want to start your next season.

The Build #141 17 to 25

The three most important questions we answer in life will be answered between the ages of 17 to 25. Here they are.

Who will you marry? What will you do for a living? Who will you serve? How important is <u>young adults ministry</u>? Do you believe that age group is in need of someone investing into their lives during this critical time? I do! Be a Kingdom leader that reaches out to these young adults and helps them navigate their way successfully.

The Build #142 15 Minutes Early

What if we came to church 15 minutes early and talked to people we did not know instead of only talking to the people we already know? What if everyone viewed themselves as part of the <u>greeter's department</u>? People/visitors would be so blessed and feel so welcome. I believe God would send more people our way because He would be confident they were being loved and taken care of in a special way. Kingdom leaders, you are now officially a member of the Greeter's Department. Enjoy your promotion.

The Build #143 80% Percent Of People

Are we losing teens to the world? Is the Church connecting with them in a way that earns their attention? The statistic is 80% of the people that are born again, accept Jesus Christ into their heart before the age of 18. If we do not win young people to Jesus, when are we going to win them? The odds are not good after 18, are they? <u>Teenagers</u> are desperate to find a Kingdom leader who will believe in them, spend time with them, and be proud of them. They may never voice this need, but your influence makes a difference. They need the wisdom you have gained in life to navigate this world. Think about the people that positively influenced your life at a crucial time.

The Build #144 Incredible Impact

<u>Children's ministry</u> in the local church should be thriving not surviving. When a Kingdom leader pours into a child, there is a life long impact that is made. Children are open, teachable, and quick to believe God's Word. I wonder who I would be today if Mrs. Dickerson at Calvary Baptist Church in Cullen, Louisiana had not poured into me? We must make sure that every child has someone loving them, teaching them, and making sure God's Word is impacting their life. The world is fighting for their attention.

The Build #145 Not A Band

Praise is the expression of your faith. Worship is the expression of your love for God. With that in mind, how important is the <u>praise and worship team</u> in the local church? The praise and worship team influences the atmosphere of a service in such a powerful way. By leading people into the presence of God, people will encounter the anointing that breaks every yoke. The anointing breaks anything that would keep them from receiving what the Father, Jesus, and the Holy Spirit has provided for them. We need people who completely grasp and understand the importance of leading praise and worship, not people who just want to be in a band. Talent is one thing, anointing is something completely different.

The Build 146 Precious Little Ones

<u>The nursery</u> in a local church is one of the most deficient departments. Many pastors just give up and hire someone by the hour to handle it. Regardless, whether the help is

paid or volunteer help, most of the time it is nothing more than just babysitting. It should not be this way. The nursery should be a place of ministry as much as the main service. Why can't we pray for the babies, read the Word to them, sing to them, and hold them? Why can't the nursery department be so dynamic that other churches come to your church to learn what is possible with these precious little ones?

The Build #147 5 Star Church

I have been traveling to around 50 churches a year since 2003. That is a lot of hotels. I have stayed in 1 star, 2 star, 3 star, 4 star, and 5 star hotels throughout the years. Here is a great question. What star should the Church be? What star should your church be? The ministry of helps are made up of people who want their church to be a reflection of heaven. I don't know what star heaven will be, but I know the Church should at least get a 5 star status. By the way, Kingdom leaders always think 5 star. They give great attention to detail.

The Build #148 Time To Rise

What ministry in a church should be the strongest? I believe the answer is men's ministry. When dad is right, the marriage will be right, when the marriage is right, the family will be right, when the family is right, the church will be right, and when the church is right, the Kingdom will be right. It is time for men to rise up and take the lead. When this happens, young people will see how it is done and the women will get to see their prayers answered.

The Build #149 Thank You Ladies

I believe so much of what the Church is around the world has so much to do with incredible women of God who have carried the load when so many men would not. I can tell you that in so many churches in which I preach, the Church would not be what it is without the <u>women's ministry</u>. Thank you ladies for all you do. Thank you for all of your intercession for the Church. Thank you for serving in all areas. Thank you ladies, because without you, the Kingdom would not be what it is today.

The Build #150 Bigger and Better

There is no need for anyone to tell me the Church or their church is not perfect. No church is perfect. They all have flaws. Every church has areas they do well, and areas that need improvement. Kingdom leaders do not sit back and critique God's churches. They jump right in the middle of a church and endeavor to leave it bigger and better than how they found it. They endeavor to leave the Church stronger for the next generation. Find a church and get busy.

The Build #151 Spiritual Power

I do not believe the local church is complicated. As a matter of fact, I believe a church should be three things. First and foremost, a church is **spiritual power.** A church should be all about introducing people to God their Father, Jesus their Lord and Savior, and the Holy Spirit their friend. A church should be all about introducing people to salvation, healing, the baptism of the Holy Spirit, and their Kingdom assignment. A church should be a place where people learn who they are In Christ, how to walk in love, and how to live by faith. A church should be a place where people come and every yoke in their life is broken, so that they can reach out with their faith and receive what Jesus Christ provided for them at calvary. A church is 1st - **Spiritual Power**.

The Build #152 Financial Power

A church is just three things. First and foremost, a church is spiritual power. See Build #151. Second, a church is **Financial power**. Whatever a church is called to do for the community and the world will require finances. It is time we stopped being so naive about the provision that must be acquired to fulfill vision. Finances must be strong to maintain a growing church, provide outreaches and provision for the community, support missions around the world, build bible schools in other nations, install water wells in villages throughout nations, provide orphanages for children, and the list goes on and on. God desires a church to function from a place of financial strength not weakness. It is time the Church has more than enough to do all God has called the Church to do. Kingdom leaders are passionate TITHERS and SOWERS in Kingdom churches.

The Build #153 Servant's Culture

A church is just three things. First and foremost, a church is spiritual power. See Build #151. Second, a church is financial power. See Build #152. Third, a church should have a **Servant's Culture**. We will be dumbfounded by the servant's culture that will dominate heaven. That is great, but we *need* that culture in the Church now, here on earth. We need, young and old, to be servants in the house of God. People who serve because they have a servant's heart. We need everyone doing something instead of a few people doing it all. Does your church have a servant's culture? I hope so, if not, ask God what you can do to bring the atmosphere of heaven into your church.

CHAPTER 9

Kingdom Pastors

In 2003, Laura and I left a wonderful season at Texas Bible Institute in Columbus, Texas, where we had been directors for almost 10 years. We were so excited to be launching what had been in our heart since we were married in 1987, Phillip Baker Ministries! Our heart was to take the Gospel to the world, leave churches bigger and better than how we found them, and see people healed and saved everywhere we went. We were ready and we were excited. One of the biggest questions we had to answer in those days was, where would we live? We had several options. We could easily move to Louisiana where we had family. Since the kids were 5, 3, and 1, having family close would have been so convenient. We loved San Antonio, where we had some dear friends that believed in us a great deal. To be honest, we could have moved anywhere. Because of modern convenience of travel, we could go to the world from any city. We chose Dickinson, Texas! Dickinson is in South Houston, about 30 minutes from the beaches of Galveston. We have been often asked, why did you choose Dickinson? The obvious question was, "Do you have family there?" The answer was no! "Are you guys from there?" The answer was no! Here is the answer. We moved to Dickinson, Texas because we always taught the students in TBI that you do not move to a city, but to a church. We moved to

Dickinson, Texas, because of Living Faith Outreach Church and Pastors John and Jeana Gilligan. We wanted to be in a church where we had a covenant relationship with the Pastors. Many years later, in hindsight, I can tell you that it was one of the greatest decisions we ever made. I do not know where PBM would be today without the Gilligan's. Our pastors have been a major part of our life and PBM and we will forever be grateful. Do you want to be a successful Kingdom leader? I believe you do, that is why you are reading this book. Kingdom leaders have a wonderful relationship with their pastor. I wrote this chapter so that YOU can have a growing, healthy, and blessed relationship with your pastor. Let's build.

The Build #154 Say Their Name

Have you had a pastor throughout your life that had a huge impact on you? A pastor that believed in you, taught you, encouraged you? Go ahead and say their name out loud. Right now, go ahead. The person whose name you just spoke is someone you need to reach out to this week and encourage and thank for their impact on your life. That pastor may be in heaven. They can also be honored by considering the following thought. How you treat your pastor now, is reflection of your honor and appreciation for that pastor from years ago.

The Build #155 Know his Story

A key to having a great relationship with your pastor is to know his/her story. The more you know their story, the more you will appreciate and understand their passions in life and the direction a church is heading. The more you understand their story, the more grace you will extend when you see their imperfections. After all, they are just as human as you and I. The more you know their story, the more you will love and appreciate them. Learn their story. I guarantee it will be amazing.

The Build #156 Through your Pastor

What about the vision for my church? Every church should definitely have a defined vision. Here's the thing you need to know. The vision will come through the pastor, not you. The vision will come through the pastor, not the board. The vision will come through the pastor, not the congregation. One of the greatest ways you can pray concerning your pastor is for the vision to become greater and more clear every day. Declare that your pastor is a visionary.

The Build #157 Pray For Him

A key to having a great relationship with your pastor is to pray for him. How should I pray for my pastor? A great place to start is by praying the Word of God over him. Pray for increased vision in his heart. You can pray that a plan would come into his spirit by the Holy Spirit that will bring the vision to pass. Pray for an outpouring of power in his life to go along with the plan. When you pray for your pastor, please know a blessing will be yours as well as his.

The Build #158 Sow and Reap

Whatever you sow, you will reap. (Galatians 6:7) When you connect to your pastor's vision, people will connect to your vision. When you do not connect to your pastor's vision, do not be surprised when people do not connect to yours. Sow loyalty and reap loyalty. Sow service and reap service. Sow seed and reap seed/harvest into your ministry from others. Care about another person's assignment, and God will raise people up that will care about your assignment.

The Build #159 007

It is hard to surprise a pastor. They see it coming from a mile away. I challenge you to surprise him with a blessing. Surprise him at Christmas. Surprise him on his birthday. Surprise him during pastors appreciation month. Surprise him when he's not expecting. Do not let him see it coming. Go "007" on him and bless his socks off. It will really make his year and every year.

The Build #160 Out of the Box

Do you want to really bless your pastor? Take his wife out of any "box" in which you have confined her. I know every kind of pastor's wife there is. I know the ones that preach and the ones that do not preach. I know the ones that sing and do not sing. There are pastor's wives that are administrative, loud, quiet, and on and on. I appreciate them all. Remove your expectations and let her be who God has called her to be. Your pastor will appreciate you greatly for doing so.

The Build #161 Consider Timing

Kingdom leaders should always consider timing when needing to speak to their pastor. You would be amazed at the things a pastor gets told right before they are about to step into the pulpit. I know a pastor that was told right before he was about to preach that the toilet was overflowing. Another pastor I know was approached by an elder who announced his resignation just as the pastor was walking to the pulpit to preach. Always ask yourself before you unload, "Is it a good time to do so?" There is a right time for everything.

The Build #162 Be Specific

Your pastor needs encouragement. No one is so spiritual that they do not need a sincere encouraging word every once in a while. The next time he preaches, don't just tell him that was a good message or that you enjoyed it. Be specific, what did he say that really spoke directly to you? That is how to encourage your pastor. Trust me on this.

The Build #163 They Will

A key to having a great relationship with your pastor is to promote him in the departments in which you serve. People need to hear you honor your pastor in his presence and out of his presence. When you do this, they will. Allow me to be very specific. Pastors need to be honored in the children's church, youth group, praise and worship practice, and anytime a group of people are meeting at a church function, whether he is present are not.

The Build #164 River of Creativity

Your pastor needs people around him who are full of creative ideas. Creativity is in such demand. Just remember, when giving an idea that you have, do not get offended if he does not like your idea and please do not attach (God said) to your idea. My attitude has always been, if you do not like my idea, just give me 5 more minutes and I will give you another. Every church needs a RIVER of creativity flowing through it at all time. Be a big part of that river.

The Build 165 Big Blessing

One of the things you can do for your pastor is to be a BIG BLESSING to their children. It is hard being a child of a pastor. They live under a microscope. More is expected of them, and it seems they get away with nothing. They are just like any other young person who is trying to figure out life. Take some time and invest into the children of your pastor. Love them. Believe in them. Be proud of them. Sow into them. Ask the Holy Spirit how you can help them be successful, love church, and love God during their childhood.

The Build #166 GRACE and MERCY

A Kingdom leader understands that their pastor and Jesus are not the same person. Jesus was perfect, your pastor is not. He has made mistakes and he will make mistakes. Determine in your heart that there is a GRACE and MERCY stored in you for the times you see his humanity. Pour out that grace and mercy when he makes a mistake in the same way you would want that grace and mercy when you make a mistake. The quote, "we judge others by their actions, but we want to be judged by our intentions" fits perfectly here. You and Jesus are not the same person either.

The Build #167 Shut It Down

When a Kingdom leader hears someone speak against their pastor, they quickly shut it down, not add to the conversation. In churches there will always be those who will say negative things behind the pastor's back. When they do, handle it in a way which makes it very obvious that you are the wrong person to say such things around. There is a devil in the world that hates all pastors and we must protect them every chance we get.

The Build #168 Can We Just Get Along?

One of the greatest sources of frustration in a local church for a pastor, is when hostility exists between leadership. Kingdom leaders, it is so important that you love God, love your pastor, love the people you have the honor to serve, and love your fellow leaders. There is already enough drama in a church. Leaders, please love one another, get along, prefer one another, make each other look good, help each other, pray for each other, and do not slander a fellow leader to make yourself look better to the pastor.

The Build #169 A Pastor Should Never

Kingdom leaders are TITHERS. A Pastor should never be put in a position where he has to speak to a leader in the church because they are not tithing. Remember, everything that has been provided that allows you the honor of serving/leading in the local church has been made available through the tithe of the wonderful people of the church. A leader tithes because they love the Kingdom. A leader tithes because they want their church strong. When a leader tithes, they have the standing, according to the Word, to teach and encourage others to tithe.

The Build #170 Positive Feedback

Pastors have to make many decisions throughout the year concerning the church. When you see that the decisions he makes bring about growth and increase, that is an appropriate time to let him know his decision, creativity, or idea was wonderful. Most people only hear feedback when it is negative. Be a Kingdom leader that affirms the great things your pastor does. It will reinforce and build his confidence to make even more significant decisions.

The Build #171 Names of Pastors

Take some time today and write down the names of pastors that impacted your life in a significant way. I think it would be wonderful if you also wrote them a note that expressed your appreciation and send it to them. Your note may well be the kind word that they need right at that moment. I love all these pastors who have greatly impacted my life, Pastor Charles Davis, Pastor Chris Witt, Pastor Ron Hammonds, Pastor Paul Troquille, Pastor Tommy Burchfield, Pastor Robert Dowdy and Pastor John Gilligan.

The Build #172 Give Pastor a Hug

Do you want your children to grow up and love their local church and pastor? I believe you do. Begin at an early age to teach and encourage your children to love the pastor. When you arrive at church, tell them to go find pastor and give them a hug. At home, speak kindly about your pastors in front of your children, pray for the church and pastor with your family. One more thing, never talk church business (drama) around your children. They are not mature enough to handle the imperfections of church people yet.

The Build #173 Voice Not a Vote

I have been a Kingdom leader in different churches and my mentality has always been that I have a voice, not a vote. I have many times given my respectful opinion concerning a matter to my pastor, and after I am through, I drop it and trust him to make the decision that needs to be made. When the pastor is blessed by my council, GREAT. When the pastor does not receive my council, GREAT. He is the pastor, I am not. He is the one that is the most responsible for the church, not me. Also, he may be privilege to information that I am not and that information may affect the decision being made. By the way, I have this same opinion about being on a board of a church.

CHAPTER 10

KINGDOM ASSIGNMENTS

The first book that I ever wrote was called The Move "From The Shallows Into The Deep". For those that read that book, the following chapter may look familiar to you. The reason for this is because I have included the chapter, Kingdom Assignments from The Move into this book, The Build. Why did I do this? Leadership in its purest form is when a servant, a leader discovers their Kingdom assignment and gives their life to walking it out. For this reason, I could not imagine writing The Build and not including this revelation that has impacted my life and so many others. Let's build.

Move #174 Our Kingdom Assignment

Jesus is the King, and we are His kings in the earth. This means that we have been given Kingdom authority with which to reign in this earthly domain. We also have a Kingdom anointing, and have gained access to Kingdom provision. Ultimately, this means that we have a Kingdom assignment! Your Kingdom assignment is where "moving deep" takes you.

When someone purposes in their heart to leave shallow waters behind and sets out for the deep, they immediately place themselves on a guaranteed collision course with their Kingdom assignment! Undeniably, there is no deep life without being who God has called you to be, and doing what God has called you to do. The deep life is a life lived with avowed purpose. However, contrary to the assumptions of a lot of people, fulfilling your Kingdom assignment does not mean that you must become a preacher. Most definitely not. There are more Kingdom assignments that have nothing to do with preaching, than there are Kingdom assignments that do. So, take a deep breath and relax. This chapter is not intended to persuade you to become a pastor, apostle, teacher, evangelist, or prophet. This chapter is focused on helping you recognize how God has called you to MOVE the Kingdom forward, and there are numerous ways to do just that. Let me first share a true story that will simplify the overall message of Kingdom assignment. This story involves one of my favorite moments during my world travels as an evangelist. I tell this story often in churches, and I believe it will remain with you a very long time.

A few years ago, I was ministering in Vanuatu, on the island of Port Villa, with one of my heroes, Dr. Graham Baker and his lovely wife, Irene Baker. Both of whom are credited with transforming the nation of Papua New Guinea. (I would love to tell you that we are related, but unfortunately, we only share the same last name.) Anyway, I was training pastors by day and we were holding crusades at night. We were having a great time ministering on Port Villa and many were being saved, delivered, and healed through the incredible miracles that were taking place.

One afternoon, we were able to find some free time. Dr. Graham decided that we should go visit a tiny island called Erakor. Dr. Graham felt that it would be a wonderful place to take some pictures and relax for the afternoon. Honestly, one of the best side benefits of going to the world with the Gospel of Jesus Christ, is that you get to *see* the world. Upon arriving, I discovered that Erakor was a resort with beautiful beaches, bungalows, and a nice little restaurant. This place is a paradise and that is why so many people choose to be married on Erakor.

Interestingly, I discovered that Erakor was a mission station back in the 1800's, and this is where this story turns deep. As a matter of fact, every time I go to the world with the gospel, Jesus always has a "moment" waiting for me. These momentous experiences are what take my life into deeper waters. My hope is that you also go on a mission trip one day because I promise, Jesus will have something very special waiting for you there. Then, you too will have a "moment with Jesus."

As Dr. Graham and I walked around this island, my eyes sought to take in the pristine scenery of a tiny island surrounded by crystal clear water. The great palms, with their fronds swaying in the warm breeze, and the vibrant green hues of the many ferns growing beneath. The ever-blooming array of tropical flowers, added the final touches to this masterpiece of landscape. The long stretches of soft, golden beaches were incredibly difficult to walk away from as we continued our survey of Erakor.

As we ventured deeper into the island foliage, we suddenly came upon an old, outdoor church that had no roof or walls. There were no chairs or pew benches for those who attended this church, only boards on which to sit. There was however, a pulpit from which a minister could preach the Gospel. I found it amazing that the commercial resort preserved and carefully tended to this historic site. Apparently, the people honored the great work that had been done here for the Kingdom years ago. I took some pictures of this outdoor church and was about to continue my tour of the island when I came upon a sight that stopped me in my tracks. At my feet, were two tombstones which bore engravings that changed my life forever. The following is what the tombstones read:

In loving memory of Amanda Bruce, wife of the
Rev. J.W. Mackenzie who died at Erakor, 30th April, 1893.
After 21 years of Christian work her last words were, "I know that Jesus is mine and I am His." Blessed are the dead, which die in the Lord.

In memory of Joseph A. who died Dec. 25th, 1875; Aged 13 months. Arthur who died Sep. 3rd 1878; Aged 19 months. Walter B. who died Feb. 12th, 1887; Aged 13 months. Beloved children of J.W. and Amanda Mackenzie.

After reading these engravings, I found myself wondering who these people who gave their life for the gospel were? Not only that, but who were these people who saw three of their small children die on that tiny island? Where were they from and how did they get here? What happened to J.W. Mackenzie and how many people were born again through their ministry? What miracles did they see when they ministered on Erakor? What was their inspiration to do mission work on Erakor in the first place? What had drawn them to this tiny island? I had so many questions standing there that day on Erakor. With a little research, I later discovered that these people were from Canada and that they had left their homeland behind for the mission field with no intention of ever returning. Even at this, however, I was still left with so many unanswered questions. I found comfort in the thought that their story was recorded in Heaven. I am sure you know by now that people are forgetful, but God **never** forgets. Every person who has given their life for the gospel of Jesus Christ has their story recorded in heaven for all eternity. In that somber moment, standing there gazing at these two tombstones, I smiled, as I realized that one day I would get to meet Amanda Mackenzie.

Most assuredly, I will find Amanda Mackenzie in heaven! I will find out where she lives, knock on her mansion door, introduce myself to her, and ask her to please tell me her story. What do you think her reaction will be? First, Amanda will probably want to know how I know her. This is where I will tell her that I did mission work in Vanuatu, and came across her tombstone in 2014. I believe at this point, we will sit down and she will begin the tale of her incredible life. Amanda will enjoy telling me her story, and I will be so blessed and happy to hear it. However, when the story is finished something momentous will happen. Amanda will look at me and say, "Now that you have heard my story, tell me yours?"

Honestly, I have always been focused on building God's Kingdom; but as I stood in front of those tombstones that day, I became much more committed to fulfilling my Kingdom assignment. Indeed, I will have a story worthy of telling Amanda Mackenzie, and anyone else in Heaven who gave their life for the gospel of Jesus Christ!

Now, what about you? Will you have a story to share with Amanda Mackenzie? The sad truth is that most believers do not have a story worth telling. Most of them only have a salvation story. Please do not misunderstand me, that story is extremely important. If it had not been for them asking Jesus to be Lord and Savior of their life, they would not even have the opportunity to spend eternity in Heaven. Here is something to think about though, do these believers want to spend eternity with people from all generations and every part of the world, who gave their lives for the gospel of Jesus Christ; while all they have to share is their salvation story? These believers will only be able to recount one glorious day in which they accepted Jesus as their Savior and the rest of their life will be defined by circumstances, hurts, bitterness, anger, regret, guilt, and just plain shallow living! Consider the following: when Amanda looks at you and asks you about your story, what story will you have to tell?

Your greatest story, the most epic account of your life, will always be your obedience to your Kingdom assignment. Your life's saga is your Kingdom assignment! This chapter is designed to help you understand the importance of your Kingdom assignment and also to help you discover what that entails. So, let us continue MOVING forward and deeper.

Move #175 We All Know

We have been given a great Kingdom assignment for our lives. When we say these words out loud, we either smile from ear to ear or our heads drop down in shame. We all know whether our life is in alignment with our Kingdom assignment or not. Furthermore, we all know if our life is moving the Kingdom forward or, not doing anything for the Kingdom at all. We all know the answers to these questions.

Move #176 Hot Pursuit

Life is to be lived in hot pursuit of your Kingdom assignment. We are supposed to be living in hot pursuit of **discovering** our Kingdom assignment, or living in hot pursuit of **fulfilling** our Kingdom Assignment. Get in hot pursuit. When your life is coming to an end, you will be so glad you did.

Move #177 He Knows

The Holy Spirit knows your Kingdom assignment. You will not be able to fulfill that assignment without the Holy Spirit revealing it to you. You must develop a deeper relationship with Him if you want Him to unveil your assignment to you. For He is our teacher, our guide, and our friend. The Holy Spirit is there to help you say, "Yes" to Jesus and "Yes" to your Kingdom assignment. The Holy Spirit will also help you complete your Kingdom assignment.

Move #178 Stir It Up

Praying in the Spirit stirs up your Kingdom assignment, and none of us are doing enough stirring. When we pray in our heavenly language, the language that came from us being baptized with the Holy Spirit, we are praying aloud the will of God in our life. Incredibly, this dynamic language is one of the greatest gifts ever given to the believer. Let us use it more often.

Move #179 Why People Backslide

When you lose sight of your Kingdom assignment, your spiritual life will begin to slide backwards. Many Christians have wondered why other Christians backslide? The truth is, these backsliding believers *never discovered* their Kingdom assignment, and then they abandoned the pursuit of it altogether. Your Kingdom assignment will always MOVE you towards a deeper and greater relationship with Jesus.

Move #180 Presence or Circumstances?

Your Kingdom assignment will be found in God's presence and not in the convenience of your circumstances. Your circumstances will always tell you that now is not the right time to obey God. In His Presence, you will find the answer to every question and problem that life will present along the way. So, get in His presence regardless of your circumstances.

Move #181 Who Will Bow?

You are either advancing towards the fulfillment of your Kingdom assignment or you are sliding back into your circumstances. Every day, every week, and every year knees are bowing. Your circumstances will bow to your Kingdom assignment, OR your assignment will bow to your circumstances. Who or what will bow today?

Move #182 Want Breakthrough?

When your Kingdom assignment becomes vulnerable to your life circumstances, your circumstances will be strengthened and God's Kingdom in the earth will be weakened. When you make your circumstances subject to your Kingdom assignment, there will be breakthrough in your life AND the Kingdom will be propelled forward through you. Let us move the Kingdom forward.

Move #183 There is a Bull's Eye

Your Kingdom assignment has a bull's eye on it that is clearly seen by the enemy. He may not know exactly what that assignment is, but he is more committed to you not knowing, than you are to knowing what God has called you to do with your life. Realizing that the enemy is more committed to your failure than you are to your success should be infuriating to you.

Move #184 Three Assignments

Do you truly desire to leave the shallow waters behind and set out for the deep waters beyond the horizon? To have success in The Kingdom, you must discover and walk out a relationship assignment, a Kingdom assignment, and finally, a prophetic assignment.

Move #185 Relationship Assignment

Your relationship assignment is your daily, weekly, and yearly necessity to draw closer to God your Father, Jesus your Lord, and the Holy Spirit your friend. These relationships must increase and develop. Let us draw closer this year than we did last year.

Move #186 Kingdom Assignment

Your Kingdom assignment is your active part in the advancement of God's Kingdom in the earth. Your role in the Kingdom was assigned to you before you were born. Every believer has an active part to play in the Kingdom of God.

Move #187 Prophetic Assignment

Your prophetic assignment is allowing God to touch your mouth, so that through your voice His Will can be manifested in the earth. Unless you declare, proclaim, and prophesy, what is in heaven will remain in heaven. Furthermore, unless you lift your voice, what hell has loosed in the earth, will remain on the loose.

Move #188 Who? It is a Clue.

Here is a clue to helping you discover your Kingdom assignment. Who or what touches your heart? Who or what pulls on your heart strings? I can assure you that what touches your heart is different than what touches mine. Do you feel compassion for those that are poor, hungry, lost, jailed, young, old, divorced, abused, leaders, pastors, etc? Who do you feel the most passionate about? Who do you have the most compassion for?

Move #189 What do you Hate?

I must ask you: what is your greatest pain? Everyone has experienced something in their past that caused great pain. Understand, with that pain came an intense hatred for what caused that pain. No, I am not talking about hating people. We can **never** hate people as Christians and followers of Jesus. I am referring to a person who has been sick before and now hates sickness. Likewise, the person who has been poor, now hates poverty. What is it that you hate? If you can narrow this down to a few things, you will have gained more clues to discovering your Kingdom assignment.

Move #190 What's the Problem?

Many people discuss the whereabouts of the greatest problems in church and believers love to answer this question. However, the "ministry of criticism" has not been given to the Church by Jesus Christ. As a matter of fact, the problem you see so clearly in the Church is a clue to your Kingdom assignment. So, feel free to jump right into the middle of that problem and fix it.

Move #191 Full Potential

What does "the church" look like at its fullest potential? Does your mind see a church full of children, the poor, the rich, or the hurting? Furthermore, do you see a church focused on prayer, the Word, discipleship, the world, or being debt free? What you see is another clue to your Kingdom assignment.

Move 192 A Warning

Let me give you a warning to heed as you pursue your Kingdom assignment. Be careful not to become offended when others are not passionate about your Kingdom assignment. Remember, they have something specific that they are passionate about as well. This is why the Kingdom of God is so effective. All believers are unique and their passions and Kingdom assignments are as infinite as our Heavenly Father.

Move #193 Do More of It

Look at your life and determine what part of it is being blessed by God. So many people constantly ask God to bless what they do and that is a wonderful thing. However, here is something that is equally amazing. Find out what God is blessing in your life and do more of it. What God is blessing is a clue to your Kingdom Assignment.

Move #194 Boldness

To be sure, everyone is bold somewhere. Personally, I am bold in the pulpit. Others may be bold in a business office, classroom, hospital, street or mission field. Some may be bolder with children, seniors, prisoners, and the list goes on and on. The area in which you are "bold" holds a clue to your Kingdom assignment.

Move #195 100% Guarantee

If you knew that you could not fail, what would you do to build the Kingdom? Let us take failure completely off of the board and eliminate fear altogether. If I gave you a 100% guarantee that you would succeed in whatever you set your hand to do, what would you choose to do? The answer to this question is another clue to your Kingdom assignment.

Of course, you have probably noticed that I have been asking you numerous questions in this chapter. Please understand that these are questions that I do not want answers to, because the answers are between you and Jesus. Jesus' intense desire is that you find your active part in the Kingdom. He brought this book across your path to help you accomplish that tremendous feat. His desire is that you leave behind those shallow waters, and move into the deep. In the deep you will find your Kingdom assignment, and life will become extremely purposeful. As you make a positive difference in people's lives, your life will become more significant because you will be propelling the Kingdom forward. I assure you that at the end of your life, you will want to know how significant you were and what type of legacy you are leaving behind. How sad it would be to know, in those final moments, that your life was defined by circumstances, storms, hurt, anger, and selfishness. Of course, you would prefer to graduate to Heaven with a big smile on your face, knowing what the Apostle Paul also knew in his final moments: "I have fought a good fight, I have finished my course, and I have kept the faith." (NIV, 1 Tim. 1:7)

  Additionally, the Apostle Paul knew that he had completed his Kingdom assignment. At the end of his life, Paul knew his "Confidential Kingdom File" had been given one big stamp of "`Mission Accomplished`" across the front. Personally, I want to know that I successfully executed and carried out my life's "Plan of Action." Let us determine to have an amazing story to tell in heaven to all of those who have gone before us into glory. Remember that Amanda Mackenzie is there in heaven waiting on you to drop by for some tea and a nice long chat. I pray you find Amanda in heaven, and that you tell her how her story inspired you to say "yes" to your Kingdom assignment.

My challenge is that you say "yes" to your Kingdom Assignment even though you may not know what it is yet! Say "yes" to your Kingdom assignment and MOVE into deeper waters. I want you to say "yes," knowing that the Father will pour out favor upon your life to help you complete your Kingdom assignment! Say, "Yes!"

CHAPTER 11

THE HEAVENLY VISION

One of the greatest statements in the Word of God is found in Acts 26:19. The Apostle Paul addressing King Agrippa said,

"I WAS NOT DISOBEDIENT TO THE HEAVENLY VISION."

I love this statement so much because the Apostle Paul is telling us that if he can be obedient to God's vision for his life, so can we. To be at the end of my life, have all my family around me, and be able to tell them I was not disobedient to the heavenly vision is the dream, the goal, and the joy that drives me. What about you? We can, as Kingdom leaders, fight a good fight, finish our course, and keep the faith. (2 Timothy 4:7) We can, as Kingdom leaders, be obedient to the heavenly vision. The thing is, it will not happen by accident. It must happen on purpose for a purpose. I want to share some keys the Apostle Paul left behind in Acts 26. I believe these keys will help us be obedient to who God has called us to be and to do all God has called us to do. I believe it is a wonderful way to bring this book to a close and to leave you with a challenge that I hope will stay with you for a very long time.

As the Apostle Paul stood before King Agrippa, the very first words he spoke in Acts 26:2 were,

"I think myself happy, King Agrippa."

For those Kingdom leaders that want to live in obedience to the heavenly vision, you will have to get "**HAPPY**" right in life. What do I mean by this? You will have to make a decision and determine in your heart that you are going to be happy and there is nothing the devil, people, or the world can do about it. Laura and I made a decision years ago that we would never be more happy than we are right now. I am not happier this year than I was last year and I will not be happier next year than I am this year. We have maxed out happy. This revelation has produced a reputation in the churches in which I preach, when I am introduced I am called,

The Happiest Evangelist you know

Every time I hear this phrase, it puts a big smile on my face. Here is a question for you. You are the Happiest _____ I know. Fill in the blank. Can you? When you can fill in the blank, you are on your way to finishing your course, keeping the faith, and fighting a good fight. Again, it will not happen if you do not get "**HAPPY**" right Let's build.

Build #196 I Think Myself Happy

Happiness is a choice you make, not a feeling based on circumstances, storms, or the opinions of others. As a Kingdom leader we will have many opportunities in life to experience joy because of achievements, victories, and breakthroughs. As a Kingdom leader we have many opportunities to experience disappointment because of failure, mistakes, trials and loss. Kingdom leaders rise above it all and like the Apostle Paul declared, "I think myself happy."

Build #197 What Else Do We Need?

Happiness comes from a revelation of who you are on the inside and not from what is happening on the outside. Are you born again? Are you In Christ? Are you Heaven bound? Is God your Father? Is Jesus your Lord and Savior? Is the Holy Spirit your friend? Does the agape love of God dwell in your heart? Has God given you the privilege and honor of being a Kingdom leader and helping others? Come on, what else do we need to be happy?

Build #198 Happiness is Gratitude

Happiness is gratitude that we show the Father for all He has done for us. People may ask what can they do to show the Father how much they appreciate Him? We all know we would not be alive without Him. We would not be well without Him. We would not have the life we have without Him. What we can do to show our appreciation is, **BE HAPPY**. When you are HAPPY, regardless of the circumstances of life, you show the Father you have a revelation of all He has done through His Son, Jesus Christ, and that makes Him **HAPPY**.

In Acts the 26th chapter, after the Apostle Paul declared himself happy, he went on to share his testimony with King Agrippa and those in attendance. In order for a Kingdom leader to get to the end of his life and be able to say that they were not disobedient to the heavenly vision they must get **"HAPPY"** right and they must get their **"TESTIMONY"** right in life. What does that mean to get your testimony right? Most believers do not have a testimony. They have a salvation testimony, a story of how they came to accept Jesus as their Lord and Savior and that is absolutely wonderful. A testimony, however, is not just what God brought you from, but what He called you to. Let me put it this way, many believers have a salvation testimony and all the rest is just a story. Let's Build.

Build #199 Scars to Wounds

Your story becomes a testimony when all the pain of life becomes wisdom that can be shared to bless the lives of others. A Kingdom leader's testimony is powerful when all the pain attached to the story is gone. It is when the open wound has become a scar, and the wisdom of God flows from their life and words to build people, the Kingdom, and the Church. Your testimony is not just that Jesus gave you THE WAY from hell to heaven, but also the fact that He gave you an assignment to move the Kingdom forward in the earth.

Build #200 The Greatest Platform

A Kingdom leader's testimony is the greatest platform they will ever have in life to lift up the matchless, wonderful, and holy name of Jesus Christ. The Apostle Paul could have shared so many things in that moment as he stood in front of King Agrippa. I mean, he did write two-thirds of the New Testament. What did he do? He chose to share his testimony. He shared what God brought him through, and what God brought him to. A Kingdom leader has a testimony, not just a story.

Build #201 Love and Hate

In a Kingdom leader's testimony is found the love and the hate that he will need to do all God has asked him to do. In your testimony is where your love for God will be discovered because of all He did for you. Because of what you have experienced, you will discover your love for people who are going through similar experiences now. In your testimony is also found the hate for the sin, sickness, and the attack unleashed by the enemy to destroy you. In our testimony is where we find our love for God and people and our hatred for all things hell related. When believers do not have this love and hate, they have a salvation testimony that details how they came to know Jesus, but the rest will be just a story defined by the circumstances of life.

Build #202 A Kingdom Leader Knows

We are to love God, love people, and hate sin. A person who hates nothing is probably not doing much to build the Kingdom. The person who hates sin, desires to see people forgiven. The person who hates disease, desires to see people healed. The person who hates poverty, desires to see people blessed. I hope you see that hate has just as much to do with ministry and your kingdom assignment, as does love. Who do you love? What do you hate? I should not have to say this but I better, you can't hate people and ever be a Kingdom leader. I pray this book and these questions help you define who you love and what you hate.

I want to say this again and be as clear as I can. In order to get to the end of your life and be able to say according to Acts 26:19,

"I WAS NOT DISOBEDIENT TO THE HEAVENLY VISION."

You are going to have to get **"HAPPY"** and your **"TESTIMONY"** right. Do not believe because of the things that you have experienced in your life, it is not possible?
Remember this, the Apostle Paul was the one who said these things. No one that is reading this book has faced the horrible things that the Apostle Paul faced. This man, Paul, was shipwrecked 3 times, scourged (received 40 stripes minus one) 5 times, beaten with rods three times, stoned, and betrayed by people everywhere he went - 2 Corinthians 11:23-28. If the Apostle Paul got **"HAPPY"** and his **"TESTIMONY"** right, then so can we.
God's grace is sufficient.

There is one more thing from Acts 26 that I want you to see. The Apostle Paul did not say he was obedient to the heavenly vision, he said he was not disobedient. Why did he state it this way? I believe he is speaking to something that has been in the churches for a very long time. Believers have a tendency to think that they are either obedient to God's will for their life, or, "Well, you know, God will understand. He knows my heart". Let me be more clear. At the end of your life the following will not fly if you were disobedient.

"God understands."
"Someone else did my part."
"I did not have the time."

In the end, we will have either been **OBEDIENT** or **DISOBEDIENT**. Now, the good news is that believers will know Heaven regardless, but do you really want to spend eternity in Heaven knowing you allowed circumstances and storms to define your life instead of your Kingdom assignment? What say you Kingdom leaders? I believe by now it should be clear why I wrote this book. I wrote *The Build* to help people BE who God called them to be and to DO what God called them to do. I wrote this book to help people be more than just a believer but a Kingdom leader who moves the Kingdom and His churches forward. I wrote this book to give Kingdom leaders the tools to BUILD their life, the Kingdom, the Church, their families and their business. I have one more Build for you that will end this book. I hope it is one that you will embrace and declare for many years to come.

Let's Build one last time,
Phillip Baker

Build #203 I AM

I am a believer in Christ Jesus and that is why I am so happy. I am a servant. I am a five rock servant. I have a servant's heart. I am a supernatural leader. I am not called to the shallow, but to the deep. I am a vision leader and I am defined by where I am going not where I have been. I reject VAGUE because everything I do, I do with precision and with excellence. I am a five star leader and everything I do, I do with five star excellence. I am a Kingdom leader and I love the Kingdom. I love God's churches. I love God's pastors. I love God's people. I hate anything from the pit of hell that would try to destroy the Kingdom and people in which Jesus Christ came and died for at Calvary. For the rest of my life I will be an instrument used by God to break containment in the lives of people and in God's Churches. At the end of my life, I will look my family in the eyes and tell them I was not disobedient to the heavenly vision, I kept the faith, I fought a good fight, and I finished my course. I will tell them, if I can do it, THEY can do it. **In Jesus Christ's Name, AMEN!**

Contact Information and Resources

To book Phillip Baker
for meetings, revivals, and seminars, contact PBM at
info@phillipbaker.org

Phillip Baker Ministries
P.O. Box 1708
Dickinson, TX 77539

www.phillipbaker.org

The Daily Move
Sign up for our FREE daily email on the website or App. The Daily Move takes 15 seconds to sign up, 10 seconds to read, but, will stay with you, MOVE you, all day! You have only expe-rienced 203 of the 730 Moves that you will get by signing up.

Made in the USA
Columbia, SC
12 August 2024